SPINNING

ADVANCE PRAISE FOR SPINNING

"A deft and moving exploration of fear, strength, and the ways in which our past lives are always catching up with our present. Janine Kovac weaves her terrifying introduction to motherhood and her career as a professional ballerina as naturally and masterfully as if she's choreographed a new dance. And she has."

—ANNA SOLOMON, author of *Leaving Lucy Pear* and co-editor of *Labor Day: True Birth Stories by Today's Best Women Writers*

"Janine Kovac has written a beautiful, honest book about what it means to live in a body, the triumphs and dangers of dancing, the deep joy and sadness of becoming a mother to twins born far too soon. I devoured this book in a single morning, wanting to know what life would unveil for this family. You will too and the story will stay with you for a long, long time after you close the book and breathe again."

—NAYOMI MUNAWEERA, author of *Island of A Thousand Mirrors* (winner of the Commonwealth Regional Prize for Asia) and *What Lies Between Us*

"I loved *Spinning* from the first page. Janine Kovac artfully weaves her past as a professional ballet dancer with the story of the premature birth of her twin sons. 'The human body has amazing healing powers if you just know how to listen to it,' writes Kovac. *Spinning* is both a testament to the miracle of the human body and to the ways that deep listening allows us to heal *and* pull meaning from our lives."

—KATE HOPPER, author of *Ready for Air: A Journey Through Premature Motherhood* and *Use Your Words: A Writing Guide for Mothers*

SPINNING

CHOREOGRAPHY *for* COMING HOME

JANINE KOVAC

AUTHOR'S NOTE:

This is a story of past events to the best of my recollection. I consulted with professionals to substantiate the medical information relayed in this book. Any medical errors are my own. For some conversations a composite character has been created to provide clarity for the reader while still preserving the integrity of the scene. Names and identifying traits of certain characters have been modified to protect the identities of those involved.

Printed in the United States of America
FIRST EDITION ISBN: 978-0-692-90494-7

Published by Moxie Road Productions
www.moxieroad.com

For my Red and Blue Babies,

My Yellow Sunshine,

And my dearest Matt

PROLOGUE

The one skill that can still be honed in a dancer's aging body is her memory. More than once I got a role simply because I was the only dancer who knew what to remember and what to push aside.

When you start to learn choreography, your mind is blank. It's at its freshest for remembering steps. This is not a good thing because choreographers change their minds. They invent combinations of turns, leaps, and lifts and often can't remember what they've done. They rely on the dancers to record and demonstrate.

Turn on the count of four.

No, wait—make it two turns.

What happens if you jump first and then turn?

Lift the left leg instead of the right.

Go back to the third version. Not that version. The one before.

Every pattern is a sequence of absolute truth. When you dance, the choreography has to look like the only version that has ever existed. The other versions lie dormant in your muscles' memory, just in case.

1

DRESS REHEARSAL

I am dozing in my bed in the hospital when I feel the pains—a gas bubble that won't go up or down. It just stays there and pulses. Maybe it's the enchiladas that I ate for lunch. Maybe it is just gas. Unfortunately, it feels sharper, closer to labor pains.

It's the day before New Year's Eve, 2009. My twins aren't due until Easter. April 10th, to be exact. Not now. Not at only twenty-five weeks and four days' gestation.

My room is bright and cheery—even when it's rainy outside, like today. There's a huge flower arrangement on the windowsill, a present from my in-laws. In the corner is a tiny plastic Christmas tree from Walgreens. Its fiber-optic branches glow from yellow to green to blue to purple. They are decorated with scraps of my daughter Chiara's preschool art, fastened to the plastic needles with paper clips my husband brought from work.

I look to my bedside table for the book my stepmom gave me about twin pregnancies. It's not there anymore. She must have given it to my nurse already. There's another woman here who has the same kind of risky pregnancy and today in the support group I told her she could have one of my books. If the book were still here, I might look up the chapter on labor. But then again, I'm in the antepartum unit, just down the hall from the labor and delivery ward. If I need expert advice, all I have to do is call the nurse.

Maybe this is a false alarm, more Braxton-Hicks contractions such as the ones I had last night. My husband Matt was fast asleep in the pullout chair. For a week now he'd been putting Chiara to sleep in her bed at home just two miles away and leaving her in the care of a relative so he could stay with me. Last week it had been my brother. This week it was my sister Jackie and stepmom Marian. Next week, it would be my mother. Matt was always careful to return home just before dawn to be with Chiara when she awoke, none the wiser.

I put my hands on my belly. It was so different from being pregnant with one child. I could feel two different energies, two different personalities almost. The nurses didn't believe me when I told them that I could tell the twins apart from how they moved inside me, but Matt did. One baby moved in flutters and zips. I called him the Red Baby. The other one seemed to mosey along, grooving to an imaginary reggae beat. I called him the Blue Baby. I could never explain why I saw those colors and not purple or green or orange, outside of the technical term for it: synesthesia. I saw colors when I read words, heard music, or felt my babies move. The Red Baby simply felt red while the Blue Baby felt blue. Just like Mozart's music was pastel pink and Prokofiev was midnight blue. Just like Chiara was a bright sunny yellow.

Usually just the warmth of my palms on my skin was enough to get the twins to dance. But this time, instead of red and blue undulations, I feel the black-and-gray streaks of a muscle spasm. A cramp. A contraction?

That's what makes this afternoon's discomfort so different from last night's. That pain felt nebulous and scattered; this feels focused, determined. Rhythmic. Pressure that momentarily interrupts my breath.

I'm not supposed to get out of bed, but if it is gas, moving around could help. I walk the few steps to my bathroom. But instead of the slow, lumbering movements I've been making of late, I'm quick, light, the way you dance on a broken foot to keep from feeling the pain.

There is a squeezing. A pull. Not the outward push of air against abdomen but abdomen against womb. No, no, no, please don't be that kind of squeezing. Not now. Not yet. Ten weeks from now, fine. Eight weeks from now—even three weeks from now. But not now.

I feel woozy, like I might slip. I hold onto the metal rail for balance and the edges of my vision go gray and fuzzy. But the center of my sight—the wastebasket, the tile floor, the edge of the sink—is all crystal clear, even though I'm not wearing my glasses. I pull on the cord labeled "Call Nurse."

Leaning against the bathroom door, I'm trying to breathe and at the same time I'm trying not to breathe. I watch myself from above—a woman with dark hair in a light green hospital gown and an enormous belly stretched taut. I can't see my face; I can only see my back. There's a tug—as if gravity is pulling me to the ground, reaching inside, and sucking life out.

Everyone thinks that an out-of-body experience means watching yourself from the rafters. That's just the visual perspective. There's also the feeling of being deeply rooted inside your vital organs, as if your heart were the center of the universe. In the same breath you observe from the outside and feel from within.

The first time I felt this was during a dress rehearsal in Germany in a ballet that was set to one of Bach's flute concertos. From the catwalks up above I watched myself dance. On the stage below I felt my arms lift and my feet point. A flurry of white chiffon in white satin pointe shoes. I was so startled I nearly tripped and took my partner down with me. But in the split second between falling and soaring

I realized I could choose to stay in this in-between land of actively moving my limbs and passively watching them. I balanced in the contradiction of the moment. It felt like flying.

When a scratchy voice comes through on the intercom I say, "I think I'm in labor."

2

BACKSTAGE

Twenty-five weeks and four days ago Matt and I sipped wine on the couch in our new home in Oakland while Chiara was tucked into her bed, sleeping soundly with Lala, her favorite doll. It was the Fourth of July. We couldn't see the fireworks, even though our apartment was on the second floor. Our living room windows faced the freeway and the kitchen windows in the back overlooked the courtyard of the ballet studio next door. But we could hear fireworks exploding on both sides of the San Francisco Bay. A soundtrack of celebration. In a week or so I'd turn forty. Next month we'd celebrate our fifth wedding anniversary and eleven years together.

We half-heartedly clinked glasses. Matt kissed me, a small peck. A consolation.

"It's better this way," he said, trying to convince himself. "Lots of kids are only children." In the past when we had talked about expanding our family the only obstacle had been the UC Berkeley calendar. I'd started school five years earlier, just days after we got married. The goal had been two kids and a college degree before my fortieth birthday.

Six weeks earlier I'd been pregnant at graduation. Memorial Day weekend. I'd stood in my cap and gown with Matt on one side and Chiara on the other. I'd been so busy with school, writing code and collecting linguistic data for my thesis, I hadn't known exactly how far along I was. Seventeen weeks? Nineteen weeks? After graduation I'd concentrate on my little Gray Baby, I'd told myself.

The doctors never called it a baby. They always referred to it as a fetus. A fetus with a high probability of congenital heart deformities. They'd know more in July, at twenty-six weeks, they said.

We didn't make it to twenty-six weeks.

The worst part wasn't the pain. Or the blood. Or the procedure that followed. The worst part was the relief. Matt and I didn't know what a congenital heart deformity would mean for a child. We were relieved that we wouldn't find out. What kind of parents did that make us?

A smattering of fireworks crackled like popcorn. Before that night we hadn't talked about what losing a baby meant for our family's future. We concentrated on follow-up appointments and other logistics. We signed the lease for the new apartment, boxed up baby clothes, bibs, and bottles as we moved across the bay from San Francisco to Oakland.

Matt sighed. He'd always pictured himself as a dad with three, four, maybe even five kids. For me, two would have been plenty. But now neither of us wanted to try again. Before, the risk of something going wrong in a pregnancy had been an abstract concept. Something you read about online. Now that we knew it could happen to us, we didn't want to take the chance that it would happen again.

"We'll be a cozy family of three," Matt said.

I nodded. He handed me a tissue and pulled me into his arms and kissed me.

Then, fireworks.

★ ★ ★ ★ ★

It was Labor Day before I made the appointment with the midwife to confirm what we had already suspected. I was pregnant again. The baby would arrive in April. If I applied to grad school this year, I'd be ready to go next fall; the baby would be four months old. The timing was perfect.

"Let's wait and see what the doctors say before we get our hopes up," Matt warned cautiously one moment, only to contradict himself in the next. "I can't believe you're pregnant! This is amazing!"

I was also hesitant to celebrate too early, but then again, what were the chances that lightning would strike twice? In quieter moments I liked to think that perhaps it was the Gray Baby growing inside me again. He or she had just waited around for a healthier body and was now was ready to come home.

Matt took the morning off from work to come with me, as he had when I was pregnant with Chiara. He squeezed my hand in his. His other hand gripped a legal pad, ready to take notes.

The room was warm; the ultrasound gel was cold. If the midwife remembered us from our appointments for the Gray Baby, she didn't show it.

"Just one heartbeat means just one head!" the midwife said with a wink. This is exactly what she'd told us last time. It got a bigger laugh then.

But now "heartbeat" made me think of "heart" which made me think of congenital deformities. I just wanted to skip to the good part, the part where she told us that our baby was healthy and perfect. But instead she pursed her lips and frowned.

"Oh, wait. No, there are two heartbeats."

That wasn't part of the script when we were here before. Last time she'd said, "Just one heartbeat means just one head." And then added,

"That's good. You don't want twins. Twins aren't just twice the work. They're sixteen times the work." To which Matt had replied, horrified, "You don't say that to the parents, do you?"

"Of course not!" she'd replied. "I just say, 'Congratulations! You're twice blessed!'"

The three of us had chuckled. Oh, those poor parents of twins, I'd thought.

Apparently this time she thought it was funny to add a joke about a two-headed baby. I waited for her to say, "Just kidding!" and resume her joke about the exponential burden of twins. But she didn't.

Matt understood before I did. He smacked his thigh and bounced up and down on the balls of his feet.

"Just two, right?" he said, trying to match the midwife's comedic wits. "We don't want to be on a reality show or anything!"

He smiled so broadly he looked like he was going to burst out of his skin. He turned and raised his palm to me.

High five? Why does he want a high five? A baby with two heads was terrible news.

"We'll have to kick you out, of course. We don't do multiples here at the clinic. But I can give you the referral for a great obstetrician who does."

Multiple *babies*? Oh no. Oh no. Oh no. You have the wrong mom, I thought. I can't have twins. I have to go to grad school. I can't be the mother of three kids. Three kids under three years old. No, no, no. I can't fit that many car seats in my car.

Two tears rolled down my cheeks. Not tears of joy but tears of arithmetic. Twins equaled twice as many diapers and twice as many college funds plus sixteen times the work, half as much sleep and no more paychecks ever. I couldn't do it.

"You'll want to get a high-res ultrasound as soon as possible," she told Matt, handing him a business card. "Twin pregnancies always carry risks, especially in mothers of advanced maternal age."

She turned to me with a meek smile. "Congratulations, sweetie. You're twice blessed."

A week later we were at the obstetrician's office for a high-resolution ultrasound and genetic testing. After the normal sort of stuff—the weighing, the undressing, the confirming of twins—our sonographer began to mutter to herself.

"It's not there," she whispered.

Matt snapped to attention. "What's not there?" he asked.

"There's supposed to be a membrane," she said, looking at the monitor, which, as far as we could tell, just looked like a lot of gray static. "I can't find it. But don't worry. It's probably nothing. I'll get the doctor."

"Don't panic," I whispered as soon as she left the exam room. If it was normal to have one of these membrane things, I was sure I had one.

The sonographer returned with a bespectacled doctor who, after wiping his hands on his lab coat, promptly shook hands with Matt. He nodded at me with a firm but professional smile and squeezed a glob of clear blue gel onto my belly.

"Let's see what we have here!" He smiled cheerfully. But as he looked at the gray patches of static on the monitor, his face drooped. "You're right," he murmured to the sonographer. "There's no membrane."

Then he turned to us. "Your twins are identical," he said gravely.

He's overreacting a bit, isn't he? I thought. Identical twins were the ones who could play practical jokes and take tests for each other. If we had to go through the work and bother of raising twins, at least we'd be able to have a little fun with it.

"But they are in the same amniotic sac and share a placenta. It's very rare," he said in a way that suggested that this was not at all desirable.

It never occurred to me that a person could have more than one placenta. I just figured a womb was a womb and a placenta was a bag that babies grew in, sort of like a liner for a waterbed mattress. I pictured all those other twins, the not-rare kind, inside their personal balloons bumping up against their twin but never really touching. My babies would be different. My babies would clasp hands and suck on each other's thumbs in utero and form neural pathways that no one else would have. That didn't sound so bad.

But clearly this was awful news. Matt turned white. He squinted at the doctor and folded his arms.

"What does this mean?" he asked.

The doctor stammered and started sentences he did not finish. He looked at the ceiling. He looked at the floor. He took a deep breath but did not exhale. When he finally spoke his voice was forced, as if he were squeezing the words out of his windpipe.

"It means we cannot complete the genetic testing procedure until you speak to a specialist, someone who can tell you all the facts in case you need to make some . . ." He looked up at the ceiling again and paused before emphasizing. "*Decisions.*"

I looked at Matt. What kind of decisions?

"Some couples in your situation choose to terminate." I shut my eyes. My heart tightened.

He must have talked for several more minutes because by the time he shook Matt's hand to leave, the gel on my belly had gone from warm and sticky to dried and flaky.

Some people (like Matt) heard a doctor say, "Some couples in your situation choose to terminate" and immediately assumed the worst—there must be something wrong with the babies or dangerous for the mother. Then there were other people (me) who assumed instead that those other couples—the terminating kind—were nothing like us. They must have had extenuating circumstances. Two babies in one bag? What was the big deal? It turned out that both sorts of people turn to the Internet for answers and neither one is comforted.

The good news was that by the time we sat down with the head doctor from the High Risk Maternal/Fetal Clinic we were already armed with the grim facts.

The clinic was adorned in soft colors. Dusty pink chairs and lavender carpet were flanked by Georgia O'Keefe prints on pale green walls. It felt like an intentional misdirection, as if paintings of big flowers softened the blow of bad news that got delivered there. The head of the clinic welcomed us into his office and motioned for us to sit down. He pulled out a chair for himself and sat in front of his desk rather than behind it. More intentional misdirection, I couldn't help thinking. As if bad news sounded better in an informal setting.

"Your twins are identical," the doctor began in a soothing voice.

Matt and I nodded. We already knew this.

"But they're not just identical; they also share the same placenta and the same amniotic sac. This type of twin pregnancy happens in one out of every 35,000 pregnancies. Some say one in 60,000. But because there's only one sac, there's a fifty-fifty chance of fetal demise."

Matt and I held our breath. This, too, we already knew from last night's Internet searches. It's also how we knew that "fetal demise" was doctorspeak for "dead."

The doctor continued. "There's nothing to keep the umbilical cords—which are about three feet long—from twisting, tangling, and crimping completely. No way to keep one twin's cord from—"

He coughed. "From choking the other twin. Unfortunately, if one baby dies, there's no way to save the healthy baby." He smoothed his tie as he spoke, as if he were trying to smooth out tangled umbilical cords.

Umbilical cords are three feet long? I tuned out to let this bit of information sink in. The entire time I was pregnant with Chiara (forty weeks and four days) I often pictured her folded body inside me but I never pictured a cord longer than she was. It seems a little superfluous, thirty-six inches of cord. Why so much? Ten inches should be plenty. Fourteen at most. Three feet! It's a wonder that every baby doesn't strangle herself on her own umbilical cord. But isn't that why we call it the miracle of life? Because logically none of it seems possible? If every baby should strangle herself on that much cord but doesn't, then the likelihood that two babies might, just because they have twice as much rope, still seems just as unlikely to me. Two cords times zero chance is still zero.

The doctor continued: "A slightly crimped umbilical cord can result in compromised nourishment but a completely crimped umbilical cord means that the fetus's oxygen supply has been cut off. For this reason we deliver the babies when their chances for survival outside the womb outweigh their chances of strangling inside the womb. We'll admit you to the antepartum ward when you're at 28 weeks for 24/7 monitoring. That's not quite seven months' gestation. If you're still pregnant at 32 weeks, we'll do a mandatory C-section then."

Four weeks in the hospital? Just waiting for something bad to happen? What would Chiara do with me in the hospital for four weeks? She wasn't even three years old yet.

"The babies will likely spend some time in the neonatal intensive care unit—the NICU." He brightened for the first time in the conversation. "You'd be surprised. There's a lot we can do with three-pound babies."

I tried not to gape. I knew preemies were small babies, but I didn't know they came in three-pound versions. My laptop weighed more than three pounds. I had textbooks that weighed more than three pounds. I didn't care what technology could do these days; I didn't want any three-pound babies.

Technology would tell us if the babies were healthy. Technology would tell us when it was time for them to be born. Technology would birth them. Technology would keep them alive. I would be stripped of my power to carry them to term, stripped of my power to bring them into this world, and stripped of my ability to nurture and nurse them. If my babies were going to survive, it would only be because modern twenty-first century technology made it possible. Reflexively, I put my hands on my belly. Within the span of a week, I'd gone from midwives and candles and Kumbaya to medical interventions at every stage: the pregnancy, childbirth, and early infancy— still with no guarantees of success.

The doctor smiled and clasped his hands in his lap. Clearly this was the best news he had to offer: that modern medicine could keep tiny babies alive.

Matt and I sat perfectly still, the way you stand onstage when it's not your turn to dance, as if we didn't want the doctor to notice that we were there. If a tree falls in the forest and there's no one there to hear it…if a doctor can't see the patient in his office…is there still something wrong with her?

Too shocked to do anything but pretend that such pre-natal science fiction couldn't possibly apply to us, we asked questions to which we already knew the answers, questions that had nothing to do with fetal demise and three-pound babies.

"So, it looks like a natural birth is out of the question?"

And: "We still need to complete our genetic testing. Can we make that appointment here?"

The doctor with the soothing voice answered with a broad smile.

I swallowed the questions I really wanted to ask: How many minutes of oxygen does a baby have if his umbilical cord is completely crimped? Is that enough time to do an emergency C-section and save the babies? And what if you're wrong? What if they'd be just fine in there for 36 weeks? Aren't you making things worse by forcing me to have a C-section?

When the appointment was over, the doctor patted Matt on the back.

"Get lots of rest and try not to think about it," he advised me. "It's about the only thing you have control over."

Never tell a ballet dancer—even one who has not been on stage in over a decade—what her body can and cannot do. During the final year of my career in San Francisco I stood on the shoulders of my partner in rehearsal as he stood on a surfboard on a platform. I was the little surfer girl in a red bikini; he was the surfer dude. Instead of a safe dismount, I fell to the floor. I landed on my face. My legs bent back over my head after impact. After the emergency room technicians determined that there were no broken ribs, no broken teeth, no internal bleeding, I went back to the theater to dance in that night's performance. In Seattle, I'd danced with a concussion. In Iceland, I'd recovered from a broken foot in less than five weeks. Maybe other monoamniotic-monochorionic pregnancies were early preemie births delivered by mandatory C-sections, but I figured I could defy expectations.

Every process needs a plan. At home I made an "I Don't Want No Three-Pound Babies" to-do list:

1. Swim twice a week

2. Take naps whenever I feel like it

3. Eat healthy and take vitamins

And, just in case, I made a "What if the Doctors Are Right" to-do list:

1. Ask Mom to fly up from Texas for the month of January to help with Chiara when I'm in the hospital

2. Find out how much our insurance will cover for lengthy hospital stays

3. Find out if the hospital has WiFi

When we finally met with a doctor to complete our genetic testing, the only appointment available to us was in a town an hour north of where we lived in Oakland and two hours north of Matt's office in Cupertino.

"Normally you'd have to call us weeks in advance. However, in your high-risk situation, you can't afford to wait," the receptionist informed us. "Unfortunately, the doctor isn't in San Francisco that day; she's in our Santa Rosa office."

Matt cleared his schedule and filed a request to take a day of vacation. I made arrangements for my brother to pick up Chiara from daycare.

The Santa Rosa office was a small single-story building with its own parking lot—a drastic change from the multi-storied San Francisco hospital with its limited street parking.

"I still don't understand," Matt whispered as we waited. "If the only risk is that the babies won't make it, why do some couples terminate? Is there some kind of risk to you just being pregnant with them? Are you in danger?"

I didn't know the answer. Most of what we'd read had discussed the risk of monoamniotic-monochorionic twins dying in the womb or risks associated with being born premature but said nothing about danger to the mother.

He shook his head. "It doesn't make any sense. There must be something they aren't telling us."

The assistant who prepped me for the ultrasound looked like a grandmother from a television show with her short, curly gray hair and modest earrings. She even wore an apron over her scrubs.

"Sorry the gel's cold, hon," she apologized. "Oh, my goodness!" She pointed to the white blobs on the ultrasound monitor. "Now, isn't that the cutest thing you've ever seen? I just love twins. Let's get you some nice pictures to take home with you."

As she marked one blob "Baby A" and the other "Baby B," she

launched into an anecdote about some older relatives who were identical twins, the kind of improbable story that is made plausible through the efforts of an enthusiastic storyteller. From time to time she stopped her story to remark on how cute the blobs of gray static looked.

"They're going to be rascals! I can just tell!" She smiled and handed us a dozen ultrasound photos.

"What's in the water you people drink up here?" the doctor asked upon entering. "You're the second mono-mono Santa Rosa mom I've had this month."

"We're from Oakland," I said softly, as if to debunk the doctor's water theory.

She looked up at me and sniffed. Clearing her throat, she began her spiel—a description of what genetic testing would or would not tell us, when we could expect our results, and how I should schedule subsequent checkups for every other week.

"You have to be prepared at every ultrasound to have a dead baby," she declared, before outlining all the ways this could happen. This was a lot more detail than we were ever given with the Gray Baby. My stomach flipped.

Matt's mouth tightened into a small line and his back stiffened as if to say, "You can tell us the harsh truth. We can take it."

"There's also the possibility that your babies could be born between twenty-three weeks and twenty-five weeks and six days' gestation, just under twenty-six weeks. We call this 'the edge of viability.' Babies born this early are at risk for cerebral palsy and are susceptible to brain bleeds."

The doctor rattled off conditions that often result from such a premature birth: blindness, impaired hearing, digestive failure, neurological problems, difficulties with sensory integration. It was a long list—seventy-five percent of babies born on the edge of viability had severe to moderate physical and mental disabilities.

That was why some couples chose to terminate, I realized, because when faced with those odds, death was the preferred option. This would be echoed again in a week when I went to visit my OB-GYN. "If I went into labor at twenty-four weeks," she advised, "I'd go take a hike on Mount Tamalpais. The last place I'd go would be the hospital. You don't want that. Especially times two."

That, of course, was the same rationale Matt and I had had when we lost the Gray Baby. But to hear it from the doctor in such a cold and direct voice, almost flippant, stirred the Mama Bear in me. I looked at Matt out of the corner of my eye. I couldn't tell if he was thinking the same thing.

"Don't worry; if they're born that early, we'll still give you a choice. No one's going to make you keep babies that will have severe disabilities." She stared at me and lifted her chin. "Do you understand what I'm saying?"

There was something so completely unnatural about all of this. In the olden days women like me got pregnant and on the seventh day after fertilization, the egg split but it was too late to grow its own placenta. However, nobody knew that. Then the mother gave birth to twins and nothing bad happened, right? These babies weren't at risk for being born premature; they would only be born premature because of a mandatory C-section.

"On the other hand," the doctor shrugged. "If you want a twenty-four-weeker, I'll do it. I'm a maternal/fetal high-risk specialist. That's what I do: deliver high-risk babies." She smiled the most grandiose of self-satisfied smiles.

I added another item to my to-do lists: find a doctor with better bedside manners.

On the drive home Matt kept his eyes on the road. I looked out the window at the fields of yellow grass. The beauty of wine country contrasted with the tension within the car.

"The doctor's fifty-fifty odds are totally meaningless," he scoffed. "It's like, maybe yes, maybe no. It's as close as you can get to 'nobody knows.'"

I nodded. "And what kind of a person tells a pregnant woman that she has to be prepared at every ultrasound to have a dead baby?"

Matt sighed. "Exactly."

I pictured going to the doctor every two weeks as recommended, Matt holding my hand, both of us holding our breath. Is there a heartbeat? Are there two heartbeats? Followed by either an exhale of relief or a gush of sorrow. Would I know before the appointment the same way I knew when the Gray Baby never got a color?

"I can't do that," I said. "I can't wake up each day and think, 'Today they might die.' I just can't. I won't."

There are so many terrible outcomes and if I focus on them, if I give them breath, I will give them life. But I can't stick my head in the sand, either. These consequences need to be kept dormant, just below the surface, the way a dancer stores different versions of choreography just in case she needs to dance those steps later.

Matt counted on his fingers. "February. They have to make it to February."

"February."

We were healthy and I was still pregnant. That was today's absolute truth. That was all I had to remember.

Our new doctor gave us the results of the genetic testing with a smile and reassuring news. "You know, I delivered my first pair of mono-mono twins thirty-one years ago. On my birthday, as a matter of fact. They're still doing great. Boys. Just like your little babies."

3

IN THE SPOTLIGHT

Some dancers are great jumpers. Some are known for their pirouettes. Others can lift their legs to their ears. I was never exceptional in any of those areas, but I did have a freakish talent for balance. Not just on half-pointe—lots of dancers can balance in flat shoes—but on pointe, on the very tips of my toes.

Part of it was my shoes, which were handmade by cobblers from Freed of London. Like most professional ballet dancers, from age seventeen through the end of my career, I had pointe shoes custom-made to fit my feet. The insoles (or "shanks"), the heels, the sides, the vamps (the satin on the top of the shoe) were all cut to my specifications.

Before I'd wear them, I'd slice the shanks, shellac the inside of the tips, and darn the outside. I'd bang them on the sidewalk and squash the tops with the heel of my foot. At the end of the process, this slipper of leather, satin, canvas, and cobbler's glue would feel like a second skin.

But the real reason I could balance so well—eight counts, sometimes even sixteen counts—was because I'd discovered a secret. First, you had to push down into the floor, pressing against gravity—like plugging into a power source. Then you had to lengthen your limbs—like spokes stretching out from a central hub. That in itself wouldn't be enough because if you reached too far in a single direction you'd fall over. Instead you had to concentrate on the little black hole that would open inside you as your extremities extended outward. The eye of the storm. That's where you'd sustain your focus. Not in the legs or arms or the foundation of your pointed foot but on that spherical space in the pit of your stomach. If you could keep your attention there, you would expand and contract at the same time. You could balance forever.

★ ★ ★ ★ ★

Standing in the bathroom of my hospital room I wait for the nurse. I feel a pull to the earth while I observe from above. My dark brown hair is pulled back into a ponytail. My new, canary-yellow maternity pajamas peek out from under a light green hospital gown. I watch myself as I make my way back to the bed, careful not to lean on the IV pole as I pull it with me. I feel like a huge, onyx-black orb. Maybe it's just gas. I could jump up and down and try to fart, but my feet are cemented to the floor. Maybe I could visualize a uterus that stops contracting, the way I'd visualized sore muscles relaxing after a demanding performance.

The strands of bright colors on the plastic Christmas tree in the corner flash like warning lights as my body grips. Somewhere deep inside me a little black hole tightens like a boxer making a fist. The thin red needle of the clock on the wall ticks around. Once. Twice. Three times. A fourth rotation. A fifth.

There it is again—another squeezing. Just after the needle makes its way all around the face, the pain subsides. Five minutes apart and lasting just over a minute. That was a textbook contraction. This is definitely labor. I'm still in my second trimester.

I can't stop this. Everything I don't want to happen is happening. I want my babies to be born safely. I want the best possible outcome. But at twenty-five weeks and four days, I don't know what "best outcome" looks like. I don't know what to hope for. This is the window period—the space of time between twenty-three weeks and twenty-five weeks and six days that the doctors warned us about. My babies' brains aren't wired enough to signal the lungs when it's time for a breath, and even if they were, the lungs aren't developed enough to take one. The optic nerves aren't fully formed. Neither are the digestive systems.

If they are born today, my boys will be in the hospital for months unless they die first. And of course there is always the chance that one will survive but his brother won't. There are too many potential futures, all of them out of my control. If I follow my imagination, I will lose my balance. I have to concentrate on the black hole imploding inside me.

I text Matt to come to the hospital.

Don't panic. I type, knowing that will probably make him panic. I send another text: *It's no help if you're panicked* and *Tell my stepmom to come to the hospital. Tell my sister to stay with Chiara.* Maybe if he thinks he has a job to do, he'll be less likely to freak out.

I brace for the next contraction.

The nurse walks briskly into my room. No jokes, no wasted words. She times the next contraction herself and then murmurs into the little pager she wears around her neck. It's three o'clock in the afternoon—the end of her shift. But there's something about the way she unclips my IV and directs an orderly to bring a gurney that lets me know that she will stay with me after her shift ends, at least for a little bit. She is very solemn. This hospital delivers seven thousand babies a year. It's what they do best. But nobody wants to deliver babies who are too fragile to live.

Don't waver, I tell myself. Let the possibilities extend into the distance. Just focus on the eye of the storm.

The pain is more intense now, and when it hits I am sucked into a place that is neither out-of-body nor connected to vital organs. It's just black, like waves of squeezing tremors. When the contraction ends, I can see and hear again.

I can tell by the way the orderly has to repeat himself to the charge nurse that something is wrong. Something logistical. They can't find a place for me. They are looking for doctors. They can't find doctors. The nurse whose shift has ended has gone to find my file and I am left with the orderlies. They wheel me into a room that feels like an office. Or a cell block. I can't see anything anymore. Just black when the contractions hit and gray when they're gone.

Reach out. Focus in. Don't waver. Balance in this moment.

★　★　★　★　★

In the five and a half months of this short pregnancy I've met most of doctors at the high-risk clinic but when this doctor enters, it's a woman I have never seen before. Her voice is quick, rushed, not evenly measured. She's scratching notes on a notepad. She doesn't have my records. I need to tell her that I have to have a C-section or else the babies might die.

She asks me a question, but my mind doesn't register what it is. She stands over me, looming large like a great specter. She looks like she's standing on a file cabinet, but that can't be. My eyes must be playing tricks on me.

"Monoamniotic! Monochorionic!" I grunt.

It's the fastest way I can tell her that I have twins who are sharing a placenta and amniotic sac and that they cannot be delivered naturally; there's the risk that their umbilical cords could choke each other. It's the most important thing she needs to know.

She nods and scribbles.

"Gestational age?" she asks.

I hold up a hand to indicate that I am having a contraction. It's stronger than the others. More intense. I'm in transition now, I think. It won't be long. Reach out. Focus in. Don't waver.

The doctor waits and rephrases her question: "How far along are you?"

"Twenty-five weeks. Four days."

"Do you know the orientation of the babies?"

"Both vertex." This is what my file would tell her. I feel so proud that I know the right answer, even though I don't know what it means. But I do know from our week of twice-a-day fetal monitoring that the twins are so small they're constantly flipping around. There's very little chance that their current position is unchanged from yesterday's biophysical sonogram.

"I'm going to examine you now," she informs me. She snaps on a glove.

I feel like I'm slipping in and out of consciousness—but flipped. It's the waking moments—looking around the room, answering the doctor's questions—that feel like a dream. And it's during the intense contractions that I feel awake, alert, focused. Powerful.

This is the precipice of fear. I can feel it. It's like a shadow, a deep puddle, a tar pit. And I'm balancing on the edge. There are many things to worry about, but if I give voice to any of them, I will fall into the pit. I will lose all perspective. But I can't step too far away, either. I need to stay where I can look into that pit. I can't turn my back on reality. The twins are coming. Today. Fifteen weeks before they are due.

"You're complete," the doctor says. "Completely dilated."

Don't waver. Just focus.

The eye of the storm becomes a tiny gray dot.

I'm wheeled into the hall and there are people everywhere, rushing around like ants. I hear snippets of conversation. They are looking for the anesthesiologist. They are bringing a set of scrubs to Matt, who is waiting outside. Someone else calls the NICU. Still no anesthesiologist. I feel a surge of energy. If the contractions were the color of black, this feeling is the color of fuchsia. I recognize this sensation. This is the time to push. The babies and my body are working in tandem. I could jump on the table and shove everybody else aside. I can do this myself, I realize. In fact, my body is already pushing to give birth. I don't need anesthesia. I don't need these doctors. I don't need surgery. I can do this myself.

And then—just as suddenly as it came—the hot pink wave of adrenaline subsides. A hand rolls me over to my side, rubs the small of my back and says, "Don't move. You'll feel a little prick here." The spinal tap. I'm rolled back to a supine position. My arms are strapped down. A blue curtain is drawn between me and my belly. I return to my mantra. Don't waver. Just focus on the eye of the storm.

I can feel two pairs of hands pushing my guts aside. The first baby seems to get pulled out right away. The second baby takes much longer, as if they can't find him, as if he's tucked behind my gall bladder, playing hide-and-seek near my pancreas. Sometimes the hands stop and I think they've pulled him out. But then they start again. It feels like ten minutes, but the official hospital time of birth of the second baby is only two minutes after his brother. I can't hear anything, but the room is flooded with people. Nine more doctors and nurses, Matt tells me later. Three for each baby and another three just in case.

"I'm going to go with them," Matt says, patting me. "You did really great." His eyebrows are pulled toward each other into a little V. I'm not sure, but I think he's been holding my hand the entire time.

The anesthesiologist says soothing things to me, but I can't remember anything that he says. As soon as the words reach my ear, they're wiped away. It's all generic stuff, but it sounds authentic.

*　*　*　*　*

They told me that I wouldn't be able to move my legs for another few hours but I can already feel my feet. Of course, I think, I was a ballet dancer.

"You're wiggling your toes!" Marian exclaims.

I can't tell if my stepmom is prompting me to make a joke. If this were anyone else in my family—Jackie, my brothers, Matt, my dad— that's what they'd say to avoid the obvious: "Oh, shit. Your twins just came out of the oven three months early." But Marian doesn't look like she's trying to distract me with humor.

"Matt's with the babies in the NICU. He said you did great." She smiles and strokes my arm.

Somewhere out of my line of sight a low voice talks to another mother-to-be from behind a curtain. I can't make out all the words, but I can hear the monotonous tone of an expert telling his patient what to expect from her impending C-section.

"In a half an hour from now . . ." Something about anesthesia.

I feel resentful. Nobody gave *me* a half an hour's notice. No one told me that my arms would be strapped down or that my babies would disappear before I would see them. It doesn't occur to me that there are many reasons why someone would give a play-by-play for C-section that won't happen for another thirty minutes—such as perhaps her surgery was bumped to allow someone else to have her babies first— someone in a situation more dire than hers. Someone like me.

The doctor I did not meet until today strides over to the edge of my bed. She leans against the railing and looks at me over the top of her black-rimmed glasses. She clears her throat and begins talking in a low, monotonous voice not unlike the voice that is explaining C-sections. My babies are boys. They're in the NICU. My husband is with them. Nothing I didn't already know.

Then: "You're very lucky."

Lucky? I don't feel lucky.

"One baby was born with a double nuchal and the other was born with a true knot in his cord." She tilts her head to the side and watches me, as if she wants to add, "if we hadn't gotten them when we did..." Instead she gestures with her hand, letting it trail off, like a tour guide inviting me to finish the sentence for her.

I know from my research on umbilical cords that a "nuchal" is the term used when a baby is born with the umbilical cord around his neck. My brother was born with the cord around his neck. Sometimes it's not serious, as in my brother's case. The doctor or midwife slips it off with the flick of a finger. But in other cases the baby loses enough oxygen to have compromised mental abilities. A double nuchal must mean that it is wrapped twice. That sounds serious. And a true knot? As opposed to what? A slip knot? A false knot?

I nod. I could ask but I'm afraid to know. My legs are buzzing; the feeling is starting to come back. It feels like pins and needles. Not painful, but distracting, as if my legs are screaming. One leg is gaining feeling faster than the other.

The doctor hands me some papers and a pen.

"This is a consent form for you to sign. To say it's okay for us to give you anesthesia and that you consent to abdominal surgery and that you have been told all the risks."

"You mean the C-section I just had?" I ask.

She nods. "When lives are in danger, we do the paperwork later."

★ ★ ★ ★ ★

My postpartum room looks like a cinder block. It's gray and grimy, nothing like my bright, sunny antepartum room. I'm too woozy to complain and besides, I heard one of the nurses say that it's overcrowded and they'll have to double up some of the moms. This room may be small and gloomy but at least I have it to myself. And, like in my antepartum room, there's a pullout couch for Matt to sleep on.

"Just rest." The nurse pats the side of my bed. "You can see your babies tomorrow." She flicks off the light and closes the door behind her.

After Chiara was born I was so struck by how empty my insides were. My Yellow Baby whom I'd carried around with me for nine months like a little buddy was now out in the world. I don't want to be alone right now. I'm so afraid that I will feel that same void, the loneliness without my little peas to keep me company. I'm afraid I will shrivel up and collapse into myself. Marian has gone back to the house. Matt is somewhere on the fourth floor with the babies. The pins and needles in my legs subside as the painkillers take effect and I drift off to an angry sleep with violent dreams of blood and guts.

★ ★ ★ ★ ★

That night Matt brings pictures. The first baby—the one born with his umbilical cord wrapped twice around the neck—is bright red. His eyes are scrunched and he looks to be in mid-scream, a good sign for someone with underdeveloped lungs. His arm is the size of Matt's finger and Matt's wedding band would easily fit over the baby's wrist. It's definitely the Red Baby. I can tell.

"One pound, twelve ounces," Matt says, reading my mind. I sigh with relief. This is heavier than I'd thought he'd be.

The next picture is of the Blue Baby, the one born with the true knot in his cord. In his birth photo the Blue Baby is slumped over. His head and face are bruised and his skin looks mottled, slimy—like a raw chicken breast. I feel a pull in my belly.

"They had a hard time pulling the little guy out!" Matt exclaims. "And his brother gave him a little shiner in the womb. Sparring already!" He grins over-enthusiastically, compensating for reality.

The Blue Baby is more lump than baby. His eyes are closed and his face expressionless. My belly twitches again, the way an amputee imagines that he still has a limb. A feeling tugs at me. Love? Pity? Panic? If I identify it, if I label this emotion, I might not recover. I might just run away.

Back when I was still dancing, I'd be onstage in the middle of a pirouette—a good turn, not a lopsided one—and between the second and third rotation I'd start to fall out of it. Nothing the audience would notice; a good landing easily saved a bad turn. But in ballet, no points are given for best efforts. If it's not a triumph, it's failure. Sometimes—not always—I'd defy gravity and do the tiniest of hops and I'd pull off that third pirouette, dammit. The trick is that you have to lift in the turn before you get too lopsided to correct yourself. As soon as you acknowledge that you are falling, you fall.

If I acknowledged that my heart was sinking, if I admitted that I felt pity for my baby, I'd fall. If I didn't give this lump all the love I had, who would?

I need to pretend that I am still turning.

Matt strokes my arm. "I know it's still early." He whispers, even though it's just us. "But I was thinking we could name one of them 'Michael,' after my dad."

I know exactly what he means. "It's still early" is code for "we don't know if the twins will survive." Matt's dad has just been diagnosed with an abdominal tumor estimated to weigh over a dozen pounds. He is scheduled to have surgery three weeks from now. What if we name one of the twins "Michael" and one of the Michaels dies?

But then again, what if we arm the twins with all kinds of family names, like talismans? Names of grandpas, maiden names, middle names, giving them namesakes in order to claim them as family. To protect them.

"I was thinking the same thing," I tell him and I look through the photographs one more time. "Michael," I say, caressing the photo of the Red Baby. "And Wagner for the Blue Baby." Another family name.

"Poor little guy." I point to the Blue Baby's picture. "That's a face only a mother could love."

Two and a half miles away Chiara is chattering with Marian and Jackie. They've gone out to eat in the neighborhood. Sushi, perhaps, or maybe fancy burgers and sweet potato fries. What a stroke of luck that Matt and I invited my family to visit for New Year's. I know my sister will indulge my daughter, and Marian will make sure that she eats her vegetables and doesn't stay up too late. One less thing to worry about as I slip in and out of consciousness and Matt goes back to the NICU to watch over the boys.

I have one of my recurring dreams. I'm at the theater and I'm thrust into a role I've never rehearsed before. My pointe shoe ribbons are too short and I can't tie them. I can't find my costume. It's time to go onstage. Usually the scene is stuck in a loop, and just before I step onstage unprepared the dream rewinds to the beginning: the call to perform and all the details pointing toward disaster. Actual disaster never happens, but the dream never gets better, either. But this time I step into the spotlight and dance. I balance on one leg and turn. Three, four, five pirouettes in *arabesque*. Eight, nine, fifteen rotations. I just keep spinning and spinning.

4

NEW ROLES

The front desk of the newborn intensive care unit is a collage of holiday cards, all photos of NICU graduates at different ages. Some are toddlers, some are first-graders, some are twelve-year-olds.

This is a place where preemies go to get well, I tell myself. They go home and learn to do baby things like crawl and toddle and then they learn to do kid things like become ballerinas and Boy Scouts. My babies are here so that they'll get well. And year after year I'll be so grateful that I'll send a card to the doctors, an annual installment on a debt of gratitude.

I scan the faces on the cards. Which smiles belonged to preemies and which ones were just siblings? I can't tell the difference. Was there anyone there like my little boys? Anyone else born at just a pound and a half?

I have never been in a NICU before. There are teddy bear paintings on the walls and pastel curtains leading into each room so we can imagine that this is a nursery and not a ward of life-support machines. I know it's supposed to be comforting, but instead it makes me worried. I had pictured the NICU as something stark and serious, with nurses and doctors walking around in hazmat suits to keep everything sterile and clean. Can they stay on high alert under these soft lights?

The nurse behind the desk highlights passages on various official documents as another nurse fastens blue plastic bracelets on my wrists. One reads "Kovac 1." The other reads "Kovac 2." Each band has a unique serial number. The number will be used to pair the patient with his prescriptions. The bands designate me as the mother. For the first time I realize that Matt is already wearing an identical pair of bracelets. They must have given them to him last night when he was here.

The formalities conclude with a detailed explanation of hand-washing protocol.

"You must scrub with anti-bacterial soap for thirty seconds each time you come into the NICU," the nurse quips.

"NICU?" Matt repeats. Only he pronounces it "nee-coo."

"Nick-you," I mutter, exasperated. This the third time today I've corrected him. Why can't he remember?

Matt turns to the nurse for verification. "Is it nee-coo or nick-you? Nee-coo? Neeee-coooo?"

"NICK-you," she confirms. She motions down the hall. "Your boys are in Room 3."

We wash our hands at the sinks, lathering up to the elbows like the stick figures in the diagrams.

"Why do you keep asking that?" I whisper.

He shrugs, his eyes twinkling. "I just think 'nee-COO' sounds better. I'm hoping if I say it enough, 'nee-COO' will catch on." His explanation is so absurd I laugh out loud, which makes him smile wider. The last time he shaved was two weeks ago, but his goofy grin still shines through his scraggly beard.

The boys share a long, narrow room, one of the few in the NICU with floor-to-ceiling windows. Outside, the gray sidewalks are slick with winter rain. It's New Year's Eve today, the last day of the year. The

Campanile, the bell tower of UC Berkeley, looms large in the distance. I forgot we were so close to campus. This landmark from my daily life of the last few years feels like a friend who has come to visit. A good omen. Of the forty rooms in the NICU, this is where they put us.

As soon as I see the baby they call Kovac 2, I recognize my Blue Baby. Under the blue bilirubin lights I can hardly see the bruises. It's as if he is already healed. Isn't that what they told us? That babies are more resilient than we give them credit for?

You are not supposed to be here, I think to the Blue Baby. You are supposed to be cloaked in darkness, surrounded by water, floating in an anti-gravity environment that makes your muscles and joints strong. Human beings were never meant to live in a plastic box. Even if that plastic box keeps them alive. This is the most unnatural thing in the world.

Matt explains to me that our babies, who weigh just over a pound and a half apiece, are micro preemies. Their condition is so critical that each baby has a personal nurse who stands over him for every minute of her eight-hour shift. She is replaced by a "meal-breaker" during her half-hour lunch and both of her fifteen-minute breaks. When the boys' breathing stops or slows, the nurses adjust the dials and take notes. The boys are never left alone.

"Our first objective is to stabilize their blood pressure," the nurse says. Behind her, machines beep and hum.

The charge nurse hands me papers to sign.

"This one's a consent form for blood transfusions. This one's for banked breast milk." She hands me a pen. "Oh, and please tell Aunt Rita 'thank you' on behalf of the nurses." She motions to a card taped to the wall next to the Blue Baby's weight graph.

Thank you to the doctors and nurses who are taking care of my nephews.
Love, Aunt Rita

Aunt Rita is Matt's aunt. Aunt Rita remembers every birthday and anniversary and hosts the annual Kovac family reunion every Labor Day. But she lives in Chicago. So far away from this NICU in Oakland. I can't connect my relative-by-marriage to this here-and-now. Aunt Rita sent a card to the NICU?

"It came with the arrangement. The biggest edible bouquet I've ever seen. It was like this." The charge nurse opens her arms wide. "There were pineapples and melons carved to look like flowers. It was amazing. We devoured it in minutes."

"Even the kale is gone," pipes in the nurse from the Red Baby's corner of the room.

I can't help but think that this chain of events is out of order. Flowers in the dressing room before the show implies congratulations, success. It's too early, too early to be grateful. Grateful has an exhale in it. We are still holding our breath.

I look at the consent forms and then at the nurse.

"What would have happened if they needed a blood transfusion and I hadn't signed this form yet?" I ask.

"Well, we just gave it to them. We had to. They needed it," she says, matter-of-factly.

Another consent form after the fact. When life is on the line, I'm learning, little pink legal papers are meaningless. I purposely avoid looking at Matt. If I do, I'll see him realize what is just dawning on me: our boys have already had a round of blood transfusions. If we lock eyes, I know I'll see my fear reflected in his face. This is our new normal; we don't have time for fear. He turns away from me, too.

Instead, I look at the NICU equipment. My poor babies. What was it like for such tiny bags of skin to be stuffed with heavy liquid? Did their itty-bitty blood vessels soak up the fresh blood like sponges or did they swell from the pressure? I can see the Blue Baby's veins through his translucent skin. They don't look like blood vessels. They look like squiggles from a ballpoint pen.

This was skin that was not meant to feel air; it was meant to be submerged in some kind of mystical fluid. These eyes were not meant to see light or faces. They should be shut for three more months, seeing only what light makes its way through layers of belly and womb. And where are their souls? Are they trapped inside that baggy skin, gasping for breath or are they floating around, watching from above?

I feel myself teetering toward a black, emotional abyss. If I don't get out of here, my heart will explode.

But I haven't even seen the Red Baby yet. I try to breathe. The air feels lodged in my chest. Maybe they should have breathing machines for the parents too. Not just the babies.

The Red Baby's nurse nudges me. "If you've washed your hands, you can touch him. Put one hand on his head and the other on the soles of his feet, like this." She holds her hands up, like she's holding an imaginary loaf of bread.

"Don't make any strokes or light touches," she cautions. "It's too over-stimulating for their nervous systems. You'll know because they'll turn their heads away or put a hand up, like they're saying, 'Stop!'" She gestures to me with a firm open palm.

I open the little doors of the Red Baby's isolette and put one hand on his head, the other on his feet. So you're the guy who flitted back and forth, I think. His fingernails are pink and perfectly shaped, as if they are part of an exquisitely carved sculpture. He looks huge. I was expecting something I could hold in the palm of my hand. Twelve inches. That's a lot bigger than a kitten. Just twenty-four hours ago *two* twelve-inch things were inside me. Kicking, rolling, avoiding the ultrasound monitor.

"You should still be a fetus, but you're not," I whisper as softly as possible. I don't want the nurse to hear me. "You're a baby." I feel a swell of pride.

This is awe. Awe, I remember from my neuropsychology classes, has an amazing effect on the brain. And right now it's turning on neural circuits that release dopamine. It'll keep the fear away. If I can just hold on to this feeling, I'll never have to be scared again. Outside the window the bell tower of UC Berkeley is whispering to me. *You learned that here. You can do this.*

"Poor little thing hasn't pooped yet," the nurse informs me. "We'll give him another day and then we'll give him a suppository."

"Awww . . ." I say to the Red Baby. And then, for the benefit of the nurse I add, "I haven't pooped yet, either." She doesn't laugh at my joke. Maybe she didn't hear me.

"Well, I haven't pooped either," I repeat, this time directly to the nurse. Still no laugh. Not even a polite half-chuckle. I look for Matt. He would have laughed at my joke. He would have added to it, made it even funnier. But he's way on the other side of the room, examining the green lights on the Blue Baby's IV pole.

The Red Baby raises his palm over his face and turns his head to the side. It's the sign for me to leave but I just got here. I sneak a peak to see if his nurse is watching me, but she's looking at the monitor. I look back at the Red Baby. Remember me? I silently beg to him. I'm your mother. You don't want me to leave. You want me to stay. I promise, no more poop jokes. Don't turn away. I haven't had enough awe yet. I need more awe to get through the day.

A loud beeping sound startles me. One of the numbers on the monitor is flashing yellow. I jerk my hands out of the isolette, as if I have been caught with my hand in the cookie jar.

The Red Baby's nurse adjusts some dials.

"This is totally normal in babies of this age. It's called a de-sat. It happens all the time." Her voice is calm, nonchalant. And I feel a twinge of shame that I have over-reacted.

"He just needs a little more oxygen. Right now he's at fifty percent oxygen, which is high. When the number stops flashing, I'll lower it. Our air is only about twenty-one percent oxygen. A long time ago they gave preemies air that was a hundred percent oxygen, not realizing that in high concentrations it's actually a poison. That's why Stevie Wonder is blind. He had retinopathy of prematurity. ROP, for short. Don't worry. Your boys will get checked regularly to see if they have it. And there's a laser surgery they do nowadays to prevent blindness."

Too much oxygen is a poison? You're giving my babies *poison*? And how much is too much?

Don't think like that, the bell tower whispers. *You'll lose it.*

Instead I turn to Matt. "Did you hear that? Stevie Wonder was a preemie!" I flash my best fake smile, the one I used onstage. He jerks up and matches my enthusiasm.

"Whoa! That's amazing!" he exclaims, a little too loudly.

"You're in good company, sweetie!" I coo to the Red Baby.

The nurse shakes her head and presses a hand to her chest. "Oh. You're both handling this so we-ell!" She stretches the word "well" into two syllables.

She motions to the monitor, which has stopped flashing.

"See? All better."

All of my belongings have been moved from my antepartum room to my current one. The Christmas tree is lopsided. Its lights are unplugged. Clothes that had been folded are now in bunches from the hasty transition. Even the beautiful flowers from Matt's parents have wilted.

I'm so groggy and my brain is spinning. I try to recollect conversations from last week, when I was still pregnant, matching words I'd heard with what the boys might need, medical terms such as "surfactant" and "betamethasone." At the same time I'm trying to forget what these terms mean because it reminds me the boys' lungs are weak and that their odds are bad. Most of all, the statistics and the information emphasize how helpless we are. Everything is out of our control.

With the exception of yesterday, Chiara has come to visit me every day. She has climbed into bed with me and pushed the button that makes the bed go up and down. Sometimes she is Dr. Strawberry. She looks at my tummy and says things such as, "You are going to be okay, Miss Janine."

She is always very gentle, but today, no matter how gentle she might be, she can't crawl into bed with me. I have too many stitches. I don't want her to be frightened, but I don't know what to say that will make this feel like a normal visit. She can't go to the NICU because the H1N1 virus is plaguing the nation this flu season. Children under twelve years old are not allowed in any intensive care units. Even if the hospital did allow it, I'm not sure Matt and I would. All that big equipment and all those solemn nurses make the NICU feel scary.

I wish I knew what to say. Last spring when my belly was firm and round we'd told her that she was going to be a big sister, only to backtrack after we'd lost the Gray Baby. "The baby wasn't ready to be a baby," I'd said. It was the closest thing I could think of that still sounded like the truth. What will I say if the boys don't make it? We haven't talked about death in our house. Why would we? She's only two and a half. We don't even kill spiders. We set them free outside. Even the squashed ones.

When my family comes to see me, Chiara holds my sister's hand. They are wearing matching knee-high boots and matching bows. My sister must have dressed her. Chiara looks so huge compared to my little Red and Blue babies. She doesn't need surfactant to help her lungs breathe. She doesn't need a tube to eat. She has never needed these things and I have always taken that fact for granted.

"Where are my brudders?" she demands.

My father answers for me. As a clinical psychologist, he always knows what to say. "They are in a special place for really tiny babies. The doctors are taking good care of them."

"Did you see them? Did you see my babies?" I ask my stepmom. She nods. "They're beautiful," she answers. Her eyes are shiny.

★　★　★　★　★

I sleep. I eat. I wait for my milk to come in. Nurses check my temperature every four hours, the same schedule the boys are on. But unlike the boys who have the same nurses, I always have a different nurse. She always says the same thing, though. "You're doing so we-*ell*. Some moms can't even sit up the day after their C-section."

At this rate, I'll be able to go home within five days. I won't be just down the hall from my babies. But if I'm running a fever, they can't discharge me. Maybe I can rig something. In the movies, kids are always getting the thermometers to read hot so they can stay home from school. Elliot in *ET* puts his thermometer against the light bulb. But everything is electronic these days. It's unlikely that I could fool a nurse.

"I found this when I was cleaning up." Matt holds up a bottle cap with an inscription that reads, "We must be willing to let go of the life we want in order to have the life that is waiting for us." Another omen.

We don't talk about the boys' chances. We both know. We know we have three more months here. At least. But Matt, ever-optimistic, is beaming. "I'm just so happy," he says, as if he's breaking the news to himself.

It's New Year's Eve. It's our tenth New Year's Eve together. A decade ago—1999—we rang in the millennium at a friend's house in Pacific Heights in San Francisco because no one knew if the world would blow up—if Y2K would make all the computers fail and seize all the money in our bank accounts. Downtown San Francisco was covered in paper calendars. We'd celebrated in style, with gowns and oyster shooters and real Champagne, not that sparkling white wine stuff. When the city didn't explode, we sang from the rooftop and smoked cigars.

Ten years later we are toasting with cranberry juice in coffee mugs that have the hospital's logo printed on them.

"To our children. We have three children." Matt says this the way I would announce I've won the lottery.

"To our children." I match his smile.

*   *   *   *   *

Matt and I want to name the boys "Michael" and "Wagner," but I'm afraid to make it official. So they go a week without names.

Every afternoon I get a call in my hospital room from a cheery voice in the records department.

"Hi-iii! The birth certificates are ready for you to complete."

"My babies were born at twenty-five weeks. I'm waiting to see if they'll live before I give them names," I say in the voice I use for telemarketers.

"Ohhhhhhhh," she says softly, like a tire losing air. "Of course."

She calls again the next day.

"They might die!" I exclaim. "I can't give them family names if they're going to die."

I'm resting in my bed on the third day when it occurs to me that I'm waiting for the records department to call. I'm not sure what my excuse will be. Perhaps I'll tell her that their grandfather is going to have surgery soon. Or maybe I'll just tell her I'm not ready yet. Choosing to sign the birth certificates is the only power I have. I want to hold on to this control as long as possible.

*   *   *   *   *

The nurses have given us scent dolls, which are scraps of baby blankets sewn into little dolls that are almost the same size as the boys. The dolls look like tents, like flannel ghosts, and come in two colors: baby pink and baby blue. I am supposed to sleep with them and then put them in the isolettes so the boys will recognize my smell. During the night my dolls must have fallen off the bed because when I find them the next morning they are covered in dust and even have a few black specks on their flannel tummies.

"I found them!" I say, flicking off some lint and handing the scent dolls to Matt.

"Honey, our boys have immune systems that are so compromised they barely function," he lectures me.

"I know that," I snap.

Now, I'm not a germaphobe. But I won't touch bathroom walls or stalls, and I often wash my hands before I go to the bathroom in a public place or use a tissue to open a door, and of course, I would never ever pick up a restaurant fork that was lying directly on a table and not on a napkin. I always use my elbow to squirt the soap into my hands because, if your hands are dirty before you wash them, then the dirtiest place in the bathroom must be the squirter on the soap, right? But I had also heard that the reason we have first-world illnesses is because we don't handle enough germs. Maybe scent dolls that have been rubbed on the dirty floor of a hospital are the perfect thing to put in the isolettes of pound-and-a-half babies with no immune systems.

"I'm sure they'll be fine," I argue.

"Let's ask the nurse," Matt says, with an even, diplomatic tone.

"These fell on the floor," I casually confess to the nurse standing in front of the-baby-to-be-named-Wagner.

She stares at me. "What floor?"

"The floor of my hospital room. Can I still put them in the isolettes?"

The nurse responds in the most nonchalant way possible. So casual that it looks forced. I brace myself for her admonishment. But all she says is, "Probably not. Let's get you some new ones."

I glance at Matt, expecting him to roll his eyes in an "I-told-you-so" sort of way. But instead he purses his lips and gives me a little pat, as if to remind himself that his wife has gone crazy and cannot be trusted.

★ ★ ★ ★ ★

I'm to be discharged tomorrow morning after two weeks in the hospital—ten days in antepartum and five in postpartum. I'm still hopeful that I might get a fever tonight and will have to stay here a few more days so I can still be just down the hall from my babies.

Matt is asleep on the foldout couch in my room. He's snoring lightly but I know that the slightest sound will make him jump to attention, panicked and clumsy. I tiptoe out of the room and down to the NICU. I flash my blue bracelets to the security guard and she waves me in.

For twenty-five weeks—not even six months—my babies and I were one. *I* gave them food. *I* gave them oxygen. *I* gave them blood. Now my role is played by technology and trained professionals. The nurses are surrogate mothers. The hospital room is a giant, artificial womb. I'm just a guest.

The machines sound even louder at night with the lights dimmed. The room takes on an eerie green glow from the monitors and ventilators. The boys' nurses—new ones, not the ones I met this morning—smile but do not talk. Perhaps they sense that I am weary of introductions and chitchat.

Through the walls I hear moaning, sobbing, the uncontrollable wails of a grieving mother. Does she know we can hear her? I wait for the sobs to subside but they only get louder. They go on and on, like crashing waves tossing a ship in a storm. I wonder if she is crying because her baby died. It sounds like the cry of a mother who has lost her child.

Is that what I will sound like?

I pace slowly back and forth between the Blue Baby and the Red Baby. The machines are intrusive, but what really bothers me is the tape on my babies' skin.

There's so much tape.

There's tape to secure the breathing tubes that are crammed down the boys' throats, tape where the IVs have punctured the skin. There's tape on my babies' cheeks, chins, arms, and legs, tape on skin that is newer than newborn—skin so fragile that it bruises from the sheer burden of being alive.

I can't do anything about the breathing tubes or the IV lines. I can't do anything about the blood transfusions. But I wish I could do something about all that tape. If it stings when I pull off a Band-Aid, how much more will it hurt my babies when the nurses change the tape?

I don't know if the Red Baby is asleep, but he sure is moving a lot. If I squint, his movements look active and spunky. But if I am honest with myself, he looks jittery and frenetic. He doesn't look like a miracle of nature and science; he doesn't even look human. He looks like a bald kitten or like an alien.

I open the doors of the isolette and slide my hands inside. I put one palm on my baby's head and the other on his feet. He feels... *scared*. It's the same body language Chiara exhibits when she's scared: slightly rigid, wanting me to hold her yet pulling away from me and into herself at the same time. The Red Baby feels rigid that way. He turns his head away from me and holds his hand outstretched over his face, palm outwards. *Stop.*

I mean it when I tell Chiara she is going to be just fine. That I will make sure that nothing bad will happen to her. But I can't promise anything to my baby boys. No one—not even the experts—knows what's going to happen. All I can do is touch Michael's head and feet and cry big, sloppy tears that drop on the little plastic doors of his bed. It occurs to me that my newborn sons have gone through more in five days of life than what I've been through in forty years. I don't know if they will be all right. It occurs to me that *I* am scared too.

"Well, we'll just have to be scared together," I whisper, as if saying it aloud is all I need to do to make the feeling go away. Did Stevie Wonder's mom do this? Did she stand over her son and make promises she couldn't keep?

"Look!" the nurse points to a yellow number on the monitor. "He knows your voice! This is the oxygen-saturation number. It's going up. That's a good sign."

Suddenly, I choke. I can't do this. I have to get out of here.

I don't know how to prepare for the worst and strive for the best at the same time. I can't live in two worlds like that. Even though we're in the trenches, I have to make a plan.

There's so much that's out of our control. I have to focus on what I can manage, what is within my grasp. The boys aren't the only ones at risk. The doctors have told Matt and me that just the strain alone of a NICU stay puts a marriage in jeopardy. We need to take care of ourselves and each other. I've just had major abdominal surgery and I have a two-and-a-half-year-old at home in addition to the two babies in the hospital. Our projected outcome is not good. It is expected that our lives will crumble and there will be nothing left.

I feel like a dolphin that needs to come up for air. If I speak now, I will crack. If I crack, I won't recover.

Without answering the nurse, I turn my back on my babies and slip out of the room.

5

BRISÉ

When my brain is still and I'm not rolling through the to-do list of life, I am dancing. Specifically, I think about *brisé*, a traveling step, which translated from French means "broken." I do them to the right. To the left. To the right. To the left. *Brisé, brisé, brisé, pas de bourée. Brisé, brisé, brisé, pas de bourée.* Over and over again. Sometimes I feel my legs twitching, as if the neural patterns in my motor cortex fire but stop short of commanding limbs to obey. Sometimes I watch myself, like in a movie. My left elbow is too straight and my left shoulder is higher than the other. It's probably what the famous ballerina Eva Evdokimiva meant when, in place of a "Nice to meet you," she exclaimed to me, "You're so crooked!"

I don't know why I play this over and over in my head. I only danced this choreography once, nearly twenty years ago in El Paso. A variation from *Flower Festival from Genzano*, an ancient staple of romantic ballet, the equivalent of required reading for American Lit 101.

Sometimes I freeze-frame the movements, perfecting the dance instant by instant. *Brisé.* Stop. Shoulder rotated back to engage the rhomboid muscle under the shoulder blade. Chin lifted. Collarbones lengthening. Tilt the ear. Lift the elbow. Heel forward. Fingers relaxed but extended. Stop. Take it from the top. Maybe this time it'll be perfect. After all, if it's not perfect, what's the point?

★ ★ ★ ★ ★

At the very beginning of my career I got a job with the National Ballet of Iceland. A week after I arrived in Reykjavik, I broke my foot.

I heard it happen. We were warming up for rehearsal and instead of wearing pointe shoes during the warm-up, I'd switched to flat shoes. Uncharacteristic for me. I always wore pointe shoes for the center part of class: adagio, pirouettes, jumps. But my special order Freed pointe shoes hadn't arrived and I wanted to save the ones I'd brought with me. In the final combination before rehearsal, I did a *pique arabesque*—a step a dancer does twenty times a day. This time my left ankle collapsed. I heard a crack.

My foot was a strange shade of blue, but it wasn't too swollen to put on pointe shoes. I danced through rehearsal. Missing steps, jumping ahead of the music. The choreographer wrinkled his nose. I apologized. I didn't mention my rapidly swelling foot.

An X-ray confirmed that there were two clean breaks on my fifth metatarsal. I returned to the ballet studio on crutches.

Eva Evdokimiva, a *prima ballerina assoluta,* was coming to Reykjavik to stage the ballet *Coppélia.* The ballet master whispered in my ear that I was in line for the lead.

She was due to arrive in five weeks. I had until then to heal. Five weeks is enough time for your muscles to turn to oatmeal, enough time for the calluses that keep you on your toes to wear away. If I wanted that part in *Coppélia*, I had to find a way to stay in shape even if I couldn't stand up.

Every day I put on makeup and dressed in a leotard and tights and gave myself a workout on the floor. I didn't really know what

I was doing. I just made up a bunch of exercises and tried to make them as hard as possible. My father had told me a story once about POWs during World War II and how they shaved every day to keep up morale.

I pushed myself, filling the three-hour grayness that passed for daylight during the Icelandic winter, extending my workouts to match the lengthening days. The week before Eva was due to arrive, I was back in class with the rest of the company, jumping, leaping, turning in pointe shoes.

The human body has amazing healing powers if you just know how to listen to it.

* * * * *

On the fifth day after my C-section, Matt brings me home from the hospital. Maybe it's the momentum of the New Year or maybe it's just the post-surgery drugs, but I have energy and optimism. And a sinking feeling that it won't last unless I can develop a routine, new habits to carry me through when the inevitable emotional blackness hits me.

Like those dark days in Iceland seventeen years ago, I create a plan. I will wake up and do ten minutes of yoga every day. If I can get that dancer's feeling again, the feeling of controlling all my muscles, even the involuntary ones, then I'll summon the strength that makes grace look effortless. I'll stay one step ahead of the depression and fear that preemie textbooks predict for moms like me.

I will start wearing makeup again.

I will dress in the brightest colors I can find: fuchsia, turquoise, cobalt blue.

At the back of my closet I find an olive green shawl, a Christmas present from several years earlier. I have never worn it before. We live in a climate that requires layers and shawls don't make good layers.

But for the NICU the shawl is perfect. It will keep me warm in the chilly hospital rooms. It's big, too, which means that I can easily drape it over the breast pump for discreet pumping.

Besides, it looks kind of dressy. It doesn't occur to me as I carefully apply mascara that I am prepping myself the way I would for a performance: the stretches, the makeup, the costume. It doesn't occur to me that the shawl has replaced the role of my makeup robe—the black silk one with an embroidered Chinese dragon on the back. I bought it on tour in Canada when I was just a teenager and I wore it before every performance for the next decade and a half.

I don't see these similarities to my dancing days. To me, the makeup, the clothes, the shawl, are just part of the new routine, like the scent dolls and the hand-washing.

★ ★ ★ ★ ★

Two days after my father and stepmom fly back to El Paso, my mother arrives. It's like the changing of the guard.

"Nonna!" Chiara greets her grandmother with the biggest hug she can manage. "I have two brudders! Look!"

One of the boys' night nurses has made Chiara a little care package: a hospital band that reads "Big Sister," a preemie diaper that looks like a miniature maxi-pad, a preemie shirt, a preemie pacifier with a long nipple as narrow as a pencil, and stickers of the boys' footprints, which are scarcely bigger than my thumbprint.

My mother bites her lip. She hasn't seen the boys yet. She's only heard my updates. These baby accoutrements—so much smaller than the ordinary newborn baby gear—have caught her off guard. But she recovers quickly.

"How exciting!" she says to Chiara with exaggerated cheerfulness.

"My brudders are Mi-call and-ah Wag-o-no."

My mother shoots me a grin, a real one. She's heard the story already—how the teachers at preschool were puzzled. What was that second name? *Oregano?* Did the Kovacs really name one twin after a saint and the other after a spice? It was possible. This was Berkeley, where half the parents get their names from J.R.R. Tolkien characters and the other half pretend that that's completely normal.

I roll my mom's suitcase to the guest room.

"When Matt's sister told her kids we'd named one twin after his mom's maiden name, one of them gasped and said, 'They named him after your computer password?'"

My mom chuckles. Then she looks more closely at the care package Chiara has brought her. She picks up the shirt. "It's so tiny. Are they really this small?"

I grimace. "Smaller. Those shirts are too big for them. They're too tiny for clothes." At a foot long, they are the size of Chiara's favorite doll, the one that fits perfectly in her arms. And even though this doll matches them in height, it's still more robust-looking, with baby fat molded in plastic creases. It weighs more, too. Our babies' skin is mottled and wrinkled, as if there wasn't enough time to build baby fat.

My mom nods and shoots a sideways glance toward Chiara to see if she's listening.

"How's Mike?" she asks quickly.

She knows that Matt's dad has been diagnosed with an abdominal tumor several inches in diameter. She probably also knows that it is malignant, an inference Matt and I have not yet made. Our logic bends in the opposite direction. A tumor that big has to be benign, we've reasoned. How else can you explain Mike's relative health? The sixty-eight-year old still regularly competes in triathlons. Someone like that can't have cancer.

I shake my head. Chiara doesn't know what the word "surgery" means so I figure it's safe to say it out loud. I use a boring, even tone so she won't think to ask questions.

"Surgery is scheduled for ten days from now, just after Martin Luther King Day."

"I've been praying for him. For all you guys."

My mother doesn't elaborate, for which I'm grateful. Even on our best behavior, our conversations about God are taut. My mother, like Matt's family, is very devout. By contrast, my visits to church are limited to weddings and Christmas and aside from my prayer during labor, I can't remember the last time I had a conversation with God.

My mother and I do agree on one important point: God is not a genie. Prayer is not a list of wishes to be granted. It is not our place to ask for miracles. I know she is not praying that Mike and the boys will get better; she is praying that "His Will Be Done" with a footnote plea that "He help us accept His Decisions." And probably a side note vote for a complete recovery, just in case God is taking suggestions.

I'm not up to a discussion about it, but deep down I feel the same way. I don't want to blindly hope that the boys are healthy; I have enough information at my fingertips to know that those are very long odds. On the off chance that God does grant wishes, however, I'd just like Him to help me stop thinking about it.

My mother stands up abruptly like a soldier reporting for duty. "Okay. How can I help?"

That night we treat ourselves to dinner at our favorite sushi restaurant. Chiara has become somewhat of a little darling with the sushi chef—the little blonde girl who likes raw squid. My mother isn't quite as adventurous, but she's still game. After we eat we'll go home and put Chiara to bed. Then Matt and I will go to the hospital to visit the boys. But on the drive to the restaurant, we get a phone call.

We don't know yet that when the NICU calls and it's good news they talk so quickly they don't even say hello: "its-the-nicu-your-boys-are-fine-are-you-bringing-milk-with-you-today."

And when it's bad news they talk very slowly so you can absorb it all.

"Hello?" Pause. "Mis-sus Ko-vac?" Pause. "This…is…Dr. Barry… From the NICU." Pause. "Wagner. Had. A. Pul-mon-ary. Hemorrhage."

Pulmonary. Lungs. Hemorrhage. Bleeding. Blood. In the lungs.

Matt pulls over and turns off the car and strains to listen.

There's blood in the lungs of a one-pound baby and the doctors don't know why or how or what's going to happen.

"What should we do?" Matt asks when I hang up.

I snap into performance mode. No one will see me shake. They will only see a dancer's grace.

I shrug. "They say there's nothing we can do. They just wanted us to know. We'll stick to the plan. Sushi. Then put Chiara to bed. Then we'll go to the hospital. It's not good for her to have her schedule interrupted."

I don't tell him what I'm thinking: "If we act like it's bad then it'll be bad. If we act like it's nothing, then it will be nothing."

At the restaurant we are seated at our favorite table.

"It's the Ika Girl!" the hostess exclaims as she puts a bowl of edamame on the table. Chiara smiles shyly. She picks up a chopstick and pokes at the green pods.

My mother pretends to read the menu. Matt's eyes dart around the restaurant. Chiara hums to herself, oblivious to the fact that her parents and her Nonna cannot make eye contact with each other. My throat closes and my chest tightens. My face is going to melt. I can't stay here. I get up from the table and try to walk as quickly but nonchalantly as possible to the restroom in the back, pulling my NICU shawl around me like a protective cape.

The single bathroom, equipped for wheelchair access, is a refuge, a place where I can be alone. I lean against the cool, black marble sink.

The "spooky bathroom," Chiara calls it, because of its dim lights and black porcelain toilet.

Looking at my reflection, I practice the words: "I used to have a son. But he died."

I rehearse different versions:

I used to have a *son*.

I *used* to have a son.

I used to have *two* sons.

I will remember this moment as a time when I still had two sons.

I used to have a son.

If I practice saying it, maybe it won't happen.

It reminds me of that Tuesday, September 2001. A colleague called me at seven o'clock in the morning, back when you would still call people on their home phones. He was freaking out.

"Do you know what's happening?" he screeched. "I don't know if I can go to work today, man! Turn on your T.V. New York is on fire!"

I had a little dusty pink television, a child's television. As soon as I clicked it on, I saw it—one smoking tower, flames coming out of the top floors.

Wow, now there's only one, I thought. One tower standing there to remind us that once upon a time there were two towers. One day I'll tell my children, "There used to be two huge towers in New York. Now there's only one."

As soon as I thought that, the second tower crumbled down to the bottom of the screen of my ten-inch television.

I used to have a son. I used to have two sons.

At home Matt puts Chiara to bed while I pump. We can't hurry or rush. We have to make this bedtime ritual just like every other night. Our little girl can't know that her parents are terrified. She won't understand. She'll freak out.

In the living room I assemble our rented breast pump. I'm supposed to pump eight to twelve times a day, but I never manage more than six. I despise the pump, and the next person who tells me, "If it hurts when you pump, you're doing it wrong," is going home with a shoe print on the forehead. I never get more than a few ounces. I've heard that other moms can fill a bottle in just ten minutes—that they can actually see squirts of milk from the suction. I only see drops. Maybe I am doing it wrong. I turn the dial all the way to its maximum. My breast pinches and twists.

Drop. Drop. Drop.

I wish I could make it hurt even more.

When we arrive at the NICU an hour later, a big beige machine is blocking the doorway of the boys' room.

"Just stand out here until we're done," the nurse tells us. "We don't want to expose you to any radiation."

This seems a little backwards to me. If there's anyone here who shouldn't be exposed to radiation, it's probably the little one-pounder with blood in his lungs.

Dr. Barry comes up behind us and reads from her clipboard in the same nonchalant voice our waiter used to read the sashimi specials.

"So far everything looks good. There was some bleeding; that's what I called you about. We always have to call the parents when something like that happens. Just in case..." Her voice trails off. Neither Matt nor I ask her to elaborate.

The beige machine is wheeled away. I wash my hands and open the doors to Wagner's isolette. He doesn't look like he's had a major emergency. He looks the same as yesterday. Little. Sort of greenish. Sort of wrinkly.

"Will it happen again?" Matt asks meekly.

Dr. Barry sighs. "Your babies are very small. Their blood vessels are thin. Their lungs aren't used to working like this. And their hearts have to work very hard."

I put my hands on Wagner's head and feet. He feels warm. If I'm scared, he'll know. He'll be scared, too. I look out the window, searching for the Berkeley bell tower to help calm me, but it's nighttime and all I can see in the window is my own reflection.

Panic rises in my throat. I need to think of something. I imagine the Gray Baby talking to Wagner. *It's nice here,* the Gray Baby says. *You can decide later if you want to join me.*

"It's time to change his diaper," the nurse chirps. "Would you like to do it?"

Every four hours the boys get their temperature taken, their diapers are changed, and the sensor that monitors their oxygen-saturation rate is transferred from one ankle to the other. I'm told that if it isn't moved, the sensor can burn the skin. Some nurses put the sensors on the wrist, but our boys are too skinny and it doesn't work as well there. Matt's too jittery to change the boys' diapers. He prefers to learn about the equipment that keeps them alive.

"Did you bring any milk?" the nurse asks. "We can put some on a swab and you can clean his mouth. The breast milk is like an antiseptic. It can prevent infections."

I take out the two-ounce bottle of breast milk that I pumped earlier. Like a chemist, I fill a dropper and add drops of thin white milk to a tiny green swab. It looks like a sponge lollipop or a mop for a miniature window washer. As soon as I put the sponge near Wagner's face, he turns toward it.

"See? He can smell it. Go ahead. Put it in his mouth. Watch, he'll suck on it."

Wagner's eyes stay closed, but he opens his mouth. He looks like a baby bird waiting for a worm. When I put the sponge lollipop in his mouth, he sucks greedily, like a baby.

I look at Matt and we both gape. Our baby is acting like a baby.

Later, after I change Wagner's diaper and take his temperature, I sneak a sniff of the white cuff, the oxygen-saturation sensor. It stinks like a Little League locker room or like Matt's dirty gym socks. It actually smells like stinky feet. It's vile and victorious at the same time. There's a person inside this sack of skin and he smells like a little boy.

I have a son.

I have two sons.

And one of them has stinky feet.

I look around. No one is watching. I take Wagner's foot between my thumb and forefinger and gently push on the top of it to stretch his arches. Just in case he wants to be a ballet dancer when he grows up.

6

STAGE PRESENCE

I have a trick. When I feel tears coming, I let my jaw go slack and let my throat open. I imagine that I can fit an apple in my gullet, that my esophagus is the neck of a glass bottle that opens into my chest. Hard, clear, open. If I speak slowly enough I can get the words out without my voice cracking and betraying me.

If I were still dancing, or even if I were just able to take a ballet class again (which I can't, the incisions from the C-section are still too fresh), I wouldn't have to do anything with my throat to keep the tears away. I'd just have to stand in fifth position, knees out, shoulders down, chin up, and wait for the music to carry me, to breathe for me, to let the vibrations from the sound waves reverberate through my body and sweep away all the panic and fear. I wouldn't have to think about what comes next because my muscles would know the choreography.

First the body is calm and then the mind follows.

Unfortunately, my throat trick isn't working today. I am at the high-risk perinatal clinic. It was supposed to be a prenatal appointment with my obstetrician. Instead it's my two-week postpartum appointment with one of the many nurses who works here. When a nurse practitioner comes in to examine me, I'm in the middle of raucous sobs. Her salmon-pink business-casual blouse feels like a cheery intrusion.

"I'm sorry. I'm having a moment," I offer, by way of apology.

"Do you want to tell me about your moment?"

I don't. But I feel obliged to let her know that these tears aren't just part of those typical postpartum episodes, although the hormones are probably contributing to the drama.

I shake my head but tell her anyway. "I'm supposed to be in my twenty-seventh week of pregnancy but my twins were born two weeks ago."

Her face changes. Her mouth drops open slightly and her eyes widen. I hate that look. It's a look of shock and pity. I turn away from the nurse to focus on the poster behind her that shows illustrations of fetuses and their footprints at different gestational ages.

"Every day your baby is inside you counts," reads the poster's caption.

"You know, I didn't want to be so knowledgeable," I tell her. "I could have lived my whole life without learning about bradys and apneas and tachycardiac episodes."

She clears her throat and starts to comfort me, then stops herself.

"How far along did you say you were when your babies were born? Twenty-seven weeks?"

"Twenty-five and four days." I don't want to exaggerate.

The nurse stands very still, as if even moving will betray her thoughts. I can tell what she's thinking. She's going over the statistics. Perhaps she's wondering if I was able to get that second shot of steroids to help with lung development. Or maybe she's remembering another mom with preemies. She can't tell me not to worry. Or that everything will be all right. We both know those would be lies.

I wish I could just teleport myself out of this room. *Brisé.* Stop. Rotate shoulder. Lift the chin. Lengthen the back. Pull in your stomach. Heel forward. Knee back. Shoulder in line with the hip. Fingers relaxed but extended. Take it from the top. *Brisé, brisé, brisé, pas de bourée.* To the right. To the left. To the right. To the left.

"You know, there's someone here who can talk to you. I'll be right back."

I don't want to talk to anybody, but I'm too close to tears to say anything. I don't want condolences. I don't want someone to tell me it's okay to be angry or validate my grief. I want a goddamn crystal ball.

I allow myself to play out a fantasy—the life of the Janine who didn't get pregnant with twins. She's taken her GREs by now and has decided where to go to grad school. In the fantasy I'm back at Berkeley studying cognitive linguistics. Maybe I'm even studying the linguistic notation that diagrams alternate outcomes.

In this case there's a Janine in the future. She has a husband and a daughter. She drops the daughter off at preschool and continues onto the Cal campus. There are other alternate realities: the one where I didn't get injured. The one where I never left Iceland and never met Matt. The possibilities float above my head like balloons. Red, yellow, green.

And then there's the anchor. The reality. Me, sitting on a thin paper sheet in my paisley-patterned yoga pants and electric blue nursing blouse, wrapped in my NICU shawl, my security blanket. My husband is at work. My daughter is at preschool. My sons are in twin incubators in a Level III NICU. No one knows what will happen to them.

This is my life. My here and now.

Those red, yellow, and green balloons are just a waste of my mental energy. In addition to imagining alternate realities, I imagine possibilities for the boys: a balloon where Wagner is blind and Michael is fine. A balloon where Michael has cerebral palsy and Wagner is fine.

Unlike my red, yellow, and green balloons, these outcomes are future possibilities, not past opportunities that will never come to pass. The thought of so many balloons is overwhelming. If I don't stop now, I'll lose it again. I visualize cutting the strings to each hypothetical scenario. I pop the balloons that have to do with the boys' future. The balloons that represent Iceland, grad school, and other fantasies—I let those float away.

By the time the nurse returns with the therapist, I'm ready to go. I don't feel like talking.

"I'm sorry," I say. "I just remembered that my parking meter has expired."

I squeeze past both of them and slip out the door.

7

BROKEN

There are forty-eight other babies in this NICU. Most of them can be left alone for twenty minutes at a time or more. Most of them share their nurse with another baby or even three other babies. Most of them can breathe by themselves. The vast majority of babies in the NICU are healthy and full term, admitted only as a precaution. They are in and out within four days. But this doesn't occur to me. The only babies I know in the NICU are my own, micro preemies who are in critical condition. This is my normal: babies who set off alarms and the nurses at their bedsides who do not smile.

We've been here for two weeks and I know that no one is thinking about when the boys will get out. That best-case scenario is still three months away—coinciding with their due date in April. Nobody says it out loud, but right now the doctors and nurses are still waiting to see if the boys will live.

My mother paces back and forth from one baby to his brother and back again. Her hands are behind her back and she is examining everything, trying to understand it.

"What's that dial for? Why did you need to adjust it? What's a pulse-ox reading? Why are those numbers in yellow but those numbers are white?"

Each question sounds like an accusation, but really she's only try-ing to learn. Her nose is so close to Wagner's ventilator that it looks like she might adjust the knob herself. Both Wagner's nurse and Mi-chael's are on high alert, the way I am when I take Chiara to a store with ceramic Christmas ornaments. I'm sure that if my mom actually does touch the equipment, Michael's nurse is going to leap over the isolette and tackle her to the floor.

The nurse at Michael's side busies herself with writing notes and wiping the monitor with anti-bacterial wipes, as if she is concentrat-ing too hard to answer my mother's questions, which leaves Wagner's nurse to field them.

"That's the dial that controls the flow of oxygen through the breathing tubes. I could see that Wagner was having a little trouble. Not enough to set off the alarms. But this will help. When his num-bers go up—we want them to stay between eighty-seven and ninety-three—I'll turn it down again. I think some numbers are in white while others are in yellow just to make it easier to read."

My mother squints at the monitor and I can tell what she's think-ing. "Why ninety-three? Why not ninety-four or ninety-five? Why not a hundred?"

When I was a kid, it used to embarrass me that my mother was so relentless, so unabashedly demanding. She's not intimidated by anybody.

Today I'm grateful she's asking the questions that I haven't had the courage to ask. I don't want the nurses to think that I doubt their abilities and I don't want to look like a worried parent. Worrying feels like a sign of weakness. I want to look strong. Nonchalance feels like being strong.

When Matt strides in, hands in loose fists and half-jogging as if he is late for an appointment, Michael's nurse uses his entrance as an excuse to ask my mom to leave.

"Only two people at the babies' side at any given time!" she says with faux cheer, escorting my mother out of the room.

"I'll go pick up Chiara and get dinner ready so you two can stay longer. Take your time," my mom tells us, as if she has not been pushed out but was leaving anyway.

My mother is two parts nightclub bouncer and one part self-sacrificing fairy godmother. A retired English teacher, she spent her days teaching, her afternoons driving her children to ballet class and soccer practice and her nights grading papers. The single-mom Superwoman who never took a day out for herself. Like Matt, she never gets more than five hours of sleep a night. I could never be a mom like that. I don't have the stamina. Plus, not getting enough sleep makes me grouchy. I'm so grateful she is here, picking up the slack in her role as Nonna Extraordinaire.

It's time to take Wagner's temperature and change his diaper. He's wearing a black eye mask today to protect his eyes from the blue lights that shine from above. The light helps bring his bilirubin levels back to normal.

Wagner's skin looks eerie under the blue lights, which is actually comforting to me. At least now I know he's supposed to look bizarre. Under normal light I can't trust my eyes. Is he yellower today? Is he splotchy or is it just my imagination?

Matt looks at the wall chart, a bar graph of Wagner's weight. It hasn't been updated in three or four days. Neither has Michael's. Later we will learn that the nurses only update the chart when there is good news and right now the boys have been losing weight.

I point to the monitor. "The colors don't mean anything special. It's just for readability," I whisper. It's a small room and both Michael's and Wagner's nurses are within earshot. It's hard to have any privacy here.

"Yeah. I know that. And there's a setting to change them, too. They're all old DOS colors. Magenta, cyan, yellow, white. Michael's night nurse told me."

"He did?"

Matt shrugs. "Yeah. I know all about this equipment." He hitches up his pants and breaks into the character of a car mechanic, although no one but me would recognize it as such.

"Yeah. See that there? That's what you call a '59 Bristol Meyers." He points to the machine that draws a scraggly image of every breath Wagner takes. They are supposed to be circles but they are only just flat ellipses.

Wagner's nurse hides a smile. She's been pretending she can't hear us but now she turns away from her paperwork.

"You guys are doing so great," she says.

Matt grins and I can tell he's about to answer in that silly voice again. I elbow him as Dr. Barry comes into the room and we both stand a little straighter, as if we are parents reporting for duty.

"You should know that we have some concerns," she begins, in lieu of a greeting. "In addition to the boys' daily doses of caffeine, which stimulate brain functions such as breathing, we're also giving them doses of ibuprofen. It's to help close the boys' PDAs."

Matt and I stifle a giggle and I know we are thinking the same thing. Public display of affection? He shakes a finger toward Wagner in his isolette, who is lying limp on his back.

"PDA, bad. No kissing in the NICU, boys."

The doctor smiles with practiced patience, like a middle school teacher waiting for the class to settle down.

"PDA stands for *patent ductus arteriosus*. The heart has four chambers: two atria and two ventricles."

My mind speeds off into a steady stream of loosely connected free-association thoughts. Atria—like atrium. The chambers of the heart are like little sunny rooms.

"The *ductus arteriosus* is a blood vessel that connects the pulmonary artery to the proximal descending aorta. In the developing fetus it allows most of the blood from the right ventricle to bypass the fetus's fluid-filled non-functioning lungs. When the fetus is born, it usually closes so that blood can support the lungs, which now have the task of breathing. Of course in your boys' case it's open as if they were still in the womb, but the lungs need to be taking in air. PDA. Don't Google it. It'll just scare you. PDAs are very common in preemies and they often close on their own."

I'm completely lost. Did she just say that the blood needs to go to the lungs? Isn't that what Wagner had? Blood in his lungs? Oh, well, I think. At least Matt's taking notes. He can explain it to me later. He got a perfect score on his ACT molecular biology exam in high school.

Matt nods his head and scribbles on his notepad. "PDA," he writes with his red pen. Followed by "Heart has four chambers" and "Don't Google."

"The PDA can be closed surgically, but of course we don't like to do surgery on babies this small, so we give them ibuprofen and see if that works."

"Ibuprofen?" I ask. "Like Advil?"

The doctor laughs. "Yup. Believe it or not, one course of good old ibuprofen closes the PDA in sixty percent of preemies and of the preemies who need another course it works on about sixty percent of those."

Matt scratches out some math on his notepad. Sixty percent of sixty percent leaves sixteen percent. Ibuprofen doesn't work on sixteen percent of the preemies who take it. Is that a high number or a low number?

The doctor looks from Matt to me and back to Matt again. She's waiting for us to ask the obvious: "What happens if the ibuprofen doesn't work?"

But we just stare at her. I know I'm not going to ask any questions. I've only been here for a couple of weeks, but I know how it goes.

You ask follow-up questions, you get bad news, even without Google. If my mother were here, she'd ask.

"We'll do a ligation if that doesn't work, but of course we don't want to put the boys through that if we don't need to."

I have heard this word "ligation" before but I can't remember where. It sounds like it has a Latin root. Maybe like *legato* in Italian, meaning "lengthened?" Or maybe it has a Greek root. *Ligos* sounds kind of Greek. As in "to build." Like LEGO blocks. I could just ask the doctor, but I should be able to figure out what it means just from its context. The doctor is certainly acting as if it is the sort of word that everyone knows and no explanation is necessary. Like the word "escrow." On second thought, maybe it's one of those words that everyone but me knows the definition of. Like the word "escrow."

She's still looking at us as if we are supposed to be asking questions.

"Couldn't I just drink more coffee?"

"What?"

"You said they get daily doses of caffeine. Couldn't I just drink more coffee and they could get it through the breast milk?"

The doctor's eyes widen and she manages to squeeze her laugh into a chuckle. "Oh, no!" She waves dismissively. "It doesn't work that way. There's not enough caffeine in breast milk to make a difference."

"Well, then! I guess I can stop drinking those triple-shot lattes."

The doctor chuckles and cocks her head at us. "You two are handling this so well!"

The next day I break the news to Michael.

"I've got good news and bad news," I whisper, poking my nose through the little doors of his isolette. I can smell faint traces of rubbing alcohol that I have now started to associate with my babies. "The bad news is that your lungs are useless. The doctors call them 'sticky.' It means that they don't expand when you breathe. They are not strong enough."

I put my hand on his back. He is resting on his belly on what his night nurse calls "his surfboard." It's a tiny blanket folded into a long, thin cushion so that Michael can be on his tummy and his limbs can be tucked toward his belly rather than splayed out flat. They can't recreate the anti-gravity world that the boys just came from; the best they can do is rotate them. Four hours on the stomach with the head to the left. Four hours on the back. Four hours on the stomach with the head to the right. Four hours on the back.

"The good news is that you will grow new lung tissue. All the way up until you are twelve years old your body will keep growing more and more lung tissue."

Matt has a joke prepared for when the doctors tell us this. He likes to say, "So you mean right now is the best time for a baby to smoke?"

Over the last week he has repeated this joke to several different nurses with variations such as, "So what you're saying is that the best time to smoke is before you're twelve?" and "So this is the best time for our boys to smoke?"

Nobody else laughed, but I did, and that was enough for Matt. As performers we know that sometimes one laugh is all you'll get.

"Don't worry," I tell Michael. "We're not stupid. We're just terribly clever and if you ever get out of the hospital, someday you will both see for yourselves. Hang in there and keep breathing. And don't smoke. Even if you will get new lung tissue, it's against hospital regulations."

"His numbers are looking great today!" Michael's nurse gestures toward his monitor. "Would you like to hold him?"

"You mean, take him out?"

I have never held my babies before. I have never seen them outside of their isolettes. They seem so fragile, so specimen-like. It didn't even seem possible to hold them while they were in the NICU.

"I think it'll be fine," the nurse assures me. "Put the rocking chair over there and I'll hand him to you. Then I'll help you sit down." She gently takes Michael out of his isolette and gives him to me to hold.

He's lighter than I thought he'd be. He feels like a newborn kitten. His limbs are still tucked under him and his baggy diaper looks like it might fall off. His eyes are closed and he doesn't move. As soon as I press him to my chest, his head droops. He looks gray in this light. Before I can even sit down, his nurse swiftly scoops him up and puts him back in the isolette.

That's a short time to hold your baby, I think. It hasn't registered that something is very wrong.

Suddenly there are five nurses at Michael's bedside working wordlessly together, like a team of tai chi masters in a choreographed dance. One nurse fits him with a tiny green oxygen mask that she pumps by hand. Another adjusts the air pressure. A third whispers into her pager.

Nobody says, "We're losing him!" the way they do in the movies. Maybe because if everybody's thinking it, nobody needs to say it out loud.

It takes the nurses twenty minutes to stabilize him.

I look out the window at the bell tower. There has to be something that will help both of us through this moment. A thought, a breath, a gesture. Maybe something bad didn't just happen. Maybe this is just routine. If it were really serious, wouldn't I know?

8

WAITING IN THE WINGS

We have been in the NICU for almost three weeks and I have picked up a few tricks. I know that if I stand by the service elevator long enough, someone with a badge will eventually wave me in. I know that if I try to take the stairs down to the cafeteria, it will set off the fire alarm. I know that even though we're not supposed to leave things overnight in the lockers in the family lounge, we're not the only family that has claimed a cubby.

Today is Martin Luther King Day. The preschool is closed so Chiara and my mother are having a special day together. They will make hand puppets out of socks or paint with watercolors. Nonna is full of activities.

Somewhere in Florida Matt's father is being prepped for surgery. Before the eleven-hour procedure is finished, doctors will remove fifteen pounds of a malignant tumor and Mike will get several units of blood. He'll be sewn up and sent home and the doctors will call it a success. Matt and I will pat each other on the back as if we deserve the congratulations, not the doctors. All gone. All better. See? Sometimes life is easy-peasy.

I secure my purse in the locker we're not supposed to have. I wash my hands up to the elbows the way they do in the diagram above the sink. For the two hundredth time today I imagine little Michael in his sleeping state, his mind wandering and meeting up with Mike's unconsciousness three thousand miles away. Why not? Time and space can bend, can't they? Michael looks quizzically at his grandpa, who is sitting on the edge of a hospital bed with a bandage around his head even though the surgery is in his abdomen. Michael is standing like a toddler. He puts his hand on his grandpa's knee.

I make up these little fantasies because I can't unlearn what I've been told. Fifty percent of babies born at twenty-five weeks die. Fifty percent of the ones who live have major disabilities such as cerebral palsy, blindness, cognitive deficits. How much longer will we have to wait before we know if the boys will end up in the "die" group or the "live" group? These imaginary time-travel excursions make me feel as if my sons are tiny superheroes, so much more powerful than neonatology.

Dr. Barry is in the boys' room. She has a stethoscope around her neck and she is talking to the tallest nurse I've ever seen. When she sees me, she clears her throat and lifts her chin. The nurse turns away.

"We did another set of echocardiograms this morning," Dr. Barry says. The word *echocardiogram* rises and falls like a *pas de chat*. Her voice is monotone, the color of mauve.

I look at Michael in his isolette. It's time for me to change his diaper. And then I'll pump and it'll be time to change Wagner's diaper.

"The ductus between the pulmonary artery and the aorta is open," the doctor continues in her flat, mauve voice.

Pul-mon-ary. Sounds graceful. The shape of a rolling hill. By contrast, "artery" is quick, a *pas de bourée* in the middle of her sentence. Maybe I'll spend time with Michael before I pump. I'll put my hands on his head and feet and think warm thoughts.

"This time when I went to listen," she says, "I actually heard a 'whoosh.'"

Whoosh. A whoosh at the bottom of a rolling hill makes a pretty picture.

"Which means the ibuprofen didn't work. The blood vessel is still open."

Didn't work? Something didn't work? In a quick panic, I rewind the doctor's words. I subtract the colors and shapes to grasp what she is trying to say: something is wrong. Something about their hearts and their lungs and so far nothing the doctors have tried is working.

"I've scheduled the boys for ligation tomorrow. It's a very simple surgery."

Ligation. Blue. The image of a zipper. Simple surgery. Red. Cutting and stitching.

That's when it dawns on me. Ligation is sewing, as in tubal ligation. Ligation is baby heart surgery. The boys will have surgery tomorrow. All the colors disappear. My throat tightens. My chest constricts. I haven't fainted, but all I can see is white around me as if I am living in the clouds.

"We do it all the time in preemies."

Last week this doctor had said she didn't want to do surgery if she could avoid it. Her phrases feel disconnected, like the divider lines between lanes on the freeway.

"Takes ten minutes. Takes longer to prepare the patient!"

This week she's telling me it's no big deal. I was here last week. I remember what she said. Why is today so different from last week? Why can't we keep waiting?

"I can show you pictures, if you like."

Pictures of baby heart surgery? I feel as if I am spinning toward the apron of the stage, too close to the orchestra pit. If I misjudge the distance of my steps, I will fall in.

I must have teleported myself out of the boys' room because suddenly I am in the family lounge, clawing at our locker, reaching for my purse.

"Mrs. Kovac?" It's the social worker. "I have your parking passes for the hospital garage." She smiles brightly.

In a voice that is part squeak and part clipped tones, I say, "This is not a good time for me."

And then I teleport myself again into the car, driving as fast as I dare down the ramps of the parking garage, careful not to let the tires squeal on the slick pavement. I turn on the windshield wipers and only after several seconds of screeching wipers-on-dry glass do I realize it's not raining. I can't see out the window because I am crying. I thrust some bills at the parking attendant because the social worker still has my parking pass. Can the attendant see that I'm crying? Does this happen to him all day? Do lots of people leave the hospital in tears?

I'm speeding home as quickly as possible but once I'm there, I'm stuck. I can't go upstairs like this. I can't let Chiara think that anything is wrong.

Brisé, brisé, brisé, pas de bourée. To the right. Lift the chin. To the left. Heel forward. To the right. To the left. Fingers relaxed but extended. *Brisé, brisé, brisé, pas de bourée.* Stop. Take it from the top. *Brisé, brisé, brisé, pas de bourée.*

When Matt comes home, we discuss the day's schedule in whispers. He'll take a vacation day from work. Nonna will stay with Chiara. I'm surprised at how easily my husband, the workaholic, has let his job slip three or four priority notches. We used to organize our calendars around work and school, everything else filled into the empty cracks. Work was always more important for him, just as school was for me. But the day I went into antepartum, it was as if Matt forgot work completely. He still went every day, sure. But he used to arrive at seven in the morning and leave at seven at night. Now he showed up around ten and left at three. It looks as if he doesn't care about his job, but really, he doesn't have the brain space for anything but triage. After several years of being the senior paralegal at his software company, he's built up a lot of good will.

We have decided to go early to the hospital and stay the entire day, maybe even spend the night. Everything feels so uncharted. Last week the doctors didn't want to operate on Michael and Wagner because they didn't think the boys were sturdy enough. This week the boys are even more fragile, but we can't afford to wait until they improve or get stronger.

The Internet, of course, is no help. "A PDA is a hole in the heart," reads one website. I don't understand what needs to be repaired and why it will help. What does a heart valve have to do with lungs? The diagrams on Wikipedia tell me nothing. It's like a calculus problem that I can't solve. Part of me thinks that if I stare at Wikipedia long enough, the answer will appear. Another part of me remembers how that tactic never worked on my calculus exams.

The descriptions I read make surgery sound like a series of steps, like stepping stones in a path. I can't get my head around this. To me, nothing is a series of steps, everything is interconnected. Even ballet steps—maybe especially ballet steps. A *brisé* is not just a *plié* and then a *tendu* and then a jump, a beat, and a landing. It's everything working together: the position of the torso, the momentum created by two feet and followed by one foot brushing into the air. The arms, the knees, the toes, the chin. Everything works together.

I'm not going to figure out the finer points of cardio-neonatology before tomorrow. But I do understand that the brain, the heart, and the lungs are complicated systems that work together. And right now the lungs aren't strong enough to bring oxygen to the brain and the heart. The brain isn't online enough to tell the lungs and heart what to do. The heart can't do its job, either. The lungs are getting help with the ventilators. The brain is getting stimulated with caffeine. And tomorrow the heart will get the boost it needs. Three systems trying to help each other. Like the *brisé* in a *petit allegro*.

There are a million things that can go wrong when you step onto the stage. You could slip on a slick spot or a bobby pin. Your costume could tear. You might forget the choreography. You might go on stage and have the worst performance of your career. Or—everything might go great for you, but you could be dancing with others and one of them might stumble, choke, or have a wardrobe malfunction. There's so much that's out of your control. The chances are high something will go wrong. If you stop to imagine how you might fail, you will fail.

That's how you know that imagining alternative scenarios does not prepare you for them. The grace and calm that you exude must come from somewhere else. Open your ears before you step out of the wings. Let the music guide you. Trust that everything that has led up to this moment will carry you through it. And if you're wrong—if you fall or forget—you'll just have to carry on anyway so just get out there and dance.

9

OPENING NIGHT

If I could watch from above, I might see that on the morning of the surgery Matt and I are moving together in perfect synchronicity. We are on edge, but together, as if the hair on my arms is standing on end because I can feel that Matt's is the same. We are working together in a way we've never had to do before when there was just one baby and two parents. Today we are a team, perfectly hooked into each other, like corps de ballet members or synchronized swimmers.

But the surgical team, which is coming from Children's Hospital, is late and no explanations are given. They can't be stuck in traffic. Children's Hospital is less than three miles away. Did they forget? Did something go wrong?

Last month I would have ranted. I would have played the Mama Bear card the way I'd seen my own mother take a stand on the behalf of her children. "My children's lives are at stake! What's going on here?" I would have yelled.

Instead, Matt and I pace in front of the boys' room. An anger rises in me, but I don't say anything. From the outside, it looks as if we are calm and patient.

But here's the real reason I don't say what I'm thinking: a rant is a performance with cutting one-liners and specific gestures. I'm too scattered this morning to plan and practice my diatribe and I don't have the energy to pull everyone's attention to me. On the contrary, I want very much to not be seen right now, which isn't like me. As if I will jinx us if I draw attention.

Matt also tries to hide his impatience. We tell jokes instead.

"They could have walked here by now!"

"Maybe they're getting doughnuts?"

"Or hitting the anesthesia in the back room?"

Michael will go first. He's been prepped, has an IV in his tiny arm, and is wearing only a diaper. He's lying on a tiny preemie-sized gurney in Room 2 where they'll do the surgery that everyone else is calling a "procedure."

I have never seen Michael outside of his isolette and he is stunning. He looks like he is sunbathing on a tiny baby beach. For three weeks, not counting the time he passed out, I've only had a side view of him. Here he is completely stretched out and I can see his whole body all at the same time. Two arms. Two legs. One belly button. One nose. All those fingers and toes.

I put one hand on his head and the other on the soles of his feet. I pretend I have powers like Olí, the Icelandic masseuse who worked on the ballet dancers. I saw him once a week for basic maintenance. Olí was blind and spoke no English so each week I came prepared with rehearsed phrases.

Ég *ella. Hné*

I feel bad. Knee.

Ég mjög *ella. Fótur.*

I feel really bad. Ankle.

Olí wasn't like other massage therapists. He didn't have a methodical way of kneading the muscles. He'd start with his hands on the soles of the feet and he'd make odd groans as if *he* were being beaten. I'd feel jolts of electricity shooting through my feet and into my eye sockets. His touch was very light, sometimes even imperceptible. And yet I'd feel intense discomfort before feeling relaxed and wonderful. I'd arrive at Olí's limping with swollen knees and leave ready to dance another day. Muscles would contract and release. Sometimes I'd see colors—flashes of amethyst and emerald.

In the hospital I emulate Olí while I lay hands on my son. I imagine that I can feel streams of energy move from my left hand to my right through Michael's body and that it will have the same soothing and therapeutic effect on him that Olí's touch had on me. Maybe I can add a little purple and green to his little red self.

Meanwhile, I can hear the nurses in the room next door. They're with Wagner. Their snippets of conversation are "try again" and "so small" and "didn't work." From time to time Matt comes in to report on what I have already divined from eavesdropping: they are trying to find a vein for the IV, but Wagner's blood vessels are scarcely bigger than a squiggle and each one collapses under the weight and pressure of the needle.

I had planned to spend equal time with each twin before their surgeries, but by the time Wagner's prepped the nurses have decided that he can't handle any more physical stimulation.

I watch the clock. Fifteen minutes. Twenty-five minutes. Forty-five minutes. An hour. The surgical team still isn't here. My hands rest on Michael's chest and I can feel it rise into my palms with each breath. My hands grow hotter. They feel swollen, as if I'm wearing oven mitts.

There are moments when you stand next to someone, such as on your wedding day, where there is silence and tension and the air feels full. There is something very satisfying in the fullness. As if the silence is vibrating with music. As if a mother could actually transmit breath to her son through her warmth. As if a son could comfort his mother through his breath.

* ★ ★ ★ ★ ★

The surgical team is over ninety minutes late, but you wouldn't
know that from their demeanor. The surgeon struts over to us as if
he is wearing leather rock-star pants instead of dull blue scrubs. I
wait for him to explain or apologize. He doesn't. Instead he intro-
duces us to the anesthesiologist.

"We do this procedure all the time," the surgeon assures us.
"Takes ten minutes."

I don't have to look at Matt to know what he's thinking. It's the
same thing I'm thinking. It's baby heart surgery. It's okay to take longer than ten minutes. And later when we describe the day to my
mother, we will play around with alternate one-liners.

"It's a baby, not an oil change! If he takes more than ten minutes,
wouldn't that be a good thing?"

The surgeon continues. "First an incision is made along the
shoulder blade. It's very small. About an inch and a half." He shrugs
as if to emphasize that this cut is no big deal. He draws a tiny
L-shape in the air with his index finger. "That's how we get to the
heart. Through the back."

I've always thought of the heart as something in the front of the chest.
It never occurred to me that one's heart is just as close to the spine as it
is to the sternum.

The surgeon brings his other index finger up into the air.

"Then I push the lungs out of the way. We close the PDA with a
little clip." He opens his hands the way a magician shows the crowd
that the ace of hearts has disappeared. "All done!"

There are so many things that I am not thinking right now. I am
not thinking of Matt's dad Mike, his eleven-hour surgery and seventeen units of blood. I am not thinking of the frog I dissected in sev-

enth grade. I am not thinking about how mushy and flaccid the boys' bodies seem. I am not thinking of them in the same way I would step onto the stage and block out potential hazards—the safety pin in the crotch of my costume that could break open while I was dancing or the dangerous lift that had resulted in a fall during rehearsal. Those possibilities linger just beyond the boundary of my consciousness.

But I am wondering what a valve looks like. Not just a heart valve but any valve. There are trumpet valves and valves in plumbing and I cannot picture any of them. It must help with the pumping of blood. For days the nurses have been trying to describe a *patent ductus arteriosis* and I can't keep anything straight. If it's a vessel that closes shortly after birth, what does it look like? Is it fused?

Even yesterday's analogy of systems working together doesn't comfort me. What if I miss some really important bit of information because I reduced the human circulatory system to steps in a *petit allegro*?

The only thing I can keep straight is that the boys will have surgery within the hour and that this surgeon thinks it's no big deal.

"It's very simple, really," the surgeon continues. "Like putting a clip on a bag of potato chips. Blood? Sometimes there's a drop."

If Michael and Wagner's hearts are the size of their fists and their fists are the size of my thumb, how tiny is that open and flapping valve that goes whoosh? And how big is that clip?

★　★　★　★　★

We are ushered into Room 1, where Wagner waits, where the boys will recover after surgery. It is adjacent to the room where Michael is having surgery right now. A nurse has taped white paper over the glass and we cannot peer in, but we try anyway. When that fails, we tell more jokes.

"It's Ligation Wednesday! Get two ligations for the price of one!"

"Buy one ligation, get one free!"

And now we're stumped. We can't think of any other wisecracks. The surgical staff, on the other hand, can't stop laughing. We can't hear their conversation; we just hear the laughter. Is that a good thing or a bad thing? On the one hand, it does convey a certain confidence, a sense of business-as-usual. On the other hand, it also belies the focus and concentration that baby heart surgery should require.

Twelve minutes later Michael, tucked away in his isolette, is wheeled into Room 1. All we can see are the hospital baby blankets that cover the Plexiglas box. He is pushed to the back of the narrow room as Wagner is wheeled into Room 2 for his surgery.

Now the surgeon has set a precedent. We expect laughter. We expect a twelve-minute turnaround. We expect to see an isolette covered in blankets. I feel even more nervous this time. It's like nailing the big *pas de deux* lift in the first performance. What are the odds that you'll be able to execute it perfectly a second time? Are they better or worse? Are you more likely to repeat success now that you know that you can?

Or is perfection like lightning—it rarely strikes twice. For me, it was always the latter.

Michael's nurse fiddles with his monitor. She checks tubes and wires. She makes notes. She does morphine math. He'll get .188 milliliters of morphine every hour for the next two days, about two drops. And then they'll have to wean him off it. That is, if everything goes okay.

My attention is split between trying to eavesdrop on the surgeons and adding up all those drops: two drops times forty-eight hours equals ninety-six.

How much is a hundred drops of morphine?

Matt is a ball of vibration. Too freaked out to pace, too anxious to sit still, he stands near the door practically bouncing in place. Hooking up Michael's IV seems to take the nurse forever to finish. Wagner's surgery passes in a flash. Perfection repeated.

10

BALANCING ACT

When I tell people why I quit dancing, I tell them about the fall. How I'd moved from Europe to dance in San Francisco and one day in rehearsal, the director decided to try something new. What if I stood on my partner's shoulders instead of sitting on them as he balanced on a surfboard that was mounted on a two-foot-high platform? Could I do that? In ballet companies, if you want to get ahead or just keep your part, the answer is always "yes."

My partner Fausto stripped off his shirt to minimize slippage and I removed my shoes and rolled up my tights over my calves. Bare skin on bare skin. That seemed safest.

"Try it without the platform," the director suggested. "Fausto, take her by the waist and lift her onto your shoulders. Now from there take her hands. Can you climb on his shoulders from there?"

I couldn't. Sitting on Fausto's shoulders the way you might play chicken in a swimming pool didn't give me enough leverage to stand.

"Okay, climb up from behind," the director suggested. "See if that works."

Fausto crouched down and reached his arms over his head to grab my hands. I tried to climb on his back as if he were a boulder, but it didn't work. I tried again, hoisting one leg up and planting a foot directly on his shoulder, and then using the momentum to plant my weight and swing the other leg up. With shaky but strong legs Fausto stood up. I could feel him find his balance, which helped me find my own. I straightened my legs. This wasn't so hard, I thought.

"That looks great," the director grinned. "Let's try it on the board."

Fausto climbed onto the surfboard platform and extended a hand. I stood behind him and we clasped hands.

"Shouldn't someone spot her?" one of the dancers asked.

The director shook his head. "She's got this," he said with confidence.

I've got this, I repeated to myself. I swung one foot, then the other onto Fausto's shoulders. Beads of perspiration dotted his skin.

Don't look down, I thought, as I did exactly that. I could feel my center of gravity tilt when I did. It made Fausto wobble, which he used to help him wiggle back to a steady stance. His stability became my foundation. Standing tall in my black leotard and tights, I towered over the studio full of dancers, their concentration mirroring mine. I looked straight ahead, pressing down through my feet and pressing my palms into Fausto's. A solid balance feels like a moving current. It's electric.

Fausto bent his elbows as I bent my knees and prepared to dismount. Our hands were sticky.

A dancer should never look at her feet while she is dancing. It breaks the aesthetic line. It also breaks her focus.

The shift of balance was miniscule. A waver. A flicker. Like an absent-minded thought. If I had been able to teeter forward and then back, we might have found our balance again. But when I glanced at my toes sliding off Fausto's chest, now slick with sweat, I had a flash of panic.

My colleagues looked up at me as I started to fall, all of them too far away to help.

My mind flipped through the various possible scenarios. I pictured Fausto twisting on the narrow surface of the platform, contorting to catch me, his back breaking on the edge as we both toppled. I imagined him shifting to keep his balance, but falling on one foot, knee cracking as we both crashed to the floor. I envisioned myself falling forward, puncturing my sternum on the edge of the board. I saw myself falling into his arms, helpless like a fish flopping on the shore, taking him down with me.

As soon as you imagine that you are falling, you fall.

If only I'd had the courage to say, "I'm not sure what I'm doing." If only I'd been able to find the eye of the storm within my balance. If only we'd had someone spotting us. If only I hadn't imagined falling.

I pushed off Fausto's chest as if it were a diving board and he thrust my feet forward on a diagonal, propelling me past the edge of the board.

They say I flew.

I soared through the air like an acrobat. I landed on my face in a collapsed push-up. My legs bent back over my head. I never braced for impact.

If there were gasps or shrieks, I didn't hear them. If I imagine that I'm okay, I'll be okay, I thought.

Someone helped me to my feet. Someone else gave me some water to drink.

"Are you okay?"

"Are you hurt?"

"Do you want to see a doctor?"

"Do you need anything?"

"Do you think you can dance tonight?"

I answered yes to all the questions. But I went to urgent care anyway.

In the waiting room the dancer who accompanied me filled out the forms. She described the accident: "fell from a height of twelve feet onto her face."

A nurse checked for broken teeth. A doctor examined me for internal bleeding. The X-ray technician looked for broken bones. Nothing.

"Tell me again how you fell?" the doctor looked at me, puzzled.

After I described the accident, the doctor shook his head. "You could have bitten your tongue or smashed your rib cage." I couldn't tell if he thought it was miraculous or if he thought that I was exaggerating. "Yeah, sure. You can dance tonight. Come back if anything changes."

Back at the theater, I was a hero. I'd survived the most stunning of falls and didn't even have a bruise. We changed the lift, of course, but I felt like I was invincible.

I can't remember when I started to notice that I wasn't the same. If I sat for too long, my side would spasm and I'd be unable to stand or walk until the spasm subsided. It was funny at first, this cramp that made me hobble like an old lady. I could still dance. As long as I didn't sit down, I could withstand hours of rehearsals. A private Pilates instructor helped with alignment as did chiropractic visits three times a week, but something deep in my muscles was damaged.

Something else shifted, too. I told myself that the director's attention wasn't waning, that I was just being paranoid. I pretended that I avoided new lifts because I was tired, not because I'd lost the courage to try them. When my contract was up in the spring, I wasn't hired back.

Sometimes I wonder if my contract wasn't renewed because I reminded the director of this awful accident that was completely preventable. I don't know if it looked as bad as the stories I hear. I don't have my own memory of the day. The moments exist in my mind because dancers filled in the details the way parents supplement a child's memory through their anecdotes. For me, the most vivid scenes are the ones that didn't happen: Fausto, slipping, twisting, and breaking his back on the side of the board and writhing in pain. Or me, puncturing my sternum, my neck snapping back, my arms flapping behind me, throat exposed, blood. Screams. Broken bones that poke through my rib cage. Smashed bones in my wrists.

I don't tell people that, though. I spin the story a different way.

I tell them I danced through the rest of the season and that it was getting harder and harder to perform because of my age. Thirty years old is old for a dancer. That it made sense to quit when I did. I say that I'm grateful that my career-ending injury pointed me in a new direction. Worker's Compensation made it possible for me to go back to school. I learned how to code and found a job as a software engineer. I started dating this great guy named Matt, a paralegal from Tampa, Florida who danced in the *Nutcracker* every year. It's a good story. It's mostly true. But honestly, I didn't want my career to end. I wasn't ready. I keep my regret—this bitter, stone-cold feeling—carefully hidden.

11

BEHIND THE SCENES

At home Chiara is ready to perform for us. She dresses in her peach-colored ballet shoes and the shimmery orchid tutu Nonna made for her for Halloween. She will dance to *Paquita*, a classical ballet with a storyline no one remembers. It has lots of solos and variations so it's perfect for school recitals, which is where I danced it. Chiara happens to have a preference for the music that is reserved for the prima ballerina and she knows just which button to push on her Hello Kitty CD player to find it.

Her stage is the dining room, just under our gallery of photographs. There aren't many pictures. Most of the photos we have framed and hung are those given to us by friends and family. There's a portrait of Matt's parents. Baby pictures of me and another one of Matt. A photo of Chiara from her daycare. Matt and I aren't big on photographs. I have my own memory of events and often the pictures tell a different story.

"Da show is gonna start," she tells us.

Matt and I are itching to get the dishes done and put Chiara to bed so we can go back to the hospital. Since the surgeries three days ago, the twins are doing well, at least according to the doctor's expectations, but what does that mean to us? The boys are still just three-week-old babies who should be 28-week fetuses. "Doing well after surgery" still feels like a worst-case scenario.

Earlier today Wagner seemed to be in pain so his morphine was increased to two drops an hour. Pain is determined partly by watching the twins themselves and partly by the volatility of their heart rate, oxygen-saturation rate, and amount of oxygen needed. Are they really fidgety or are they calm and sleeping soundly? After they are weaned from the morphine, they'll get Tylenol suppositories. Which I'm pretty sure is just as much fun as it sounds.

The nurses tell us that the boys are doing really well. But we can't see the difference between this week and last. Last week they lay there in their isolettes getting fed through tubes in their belly buttons as if they still had umbilical cords. Sometimes they needed more oxygen; sometimes they needed less. This week they lie there getting fed through tubes in their noses and sometimes needing more oxygen and sometimes needing less. To us, "getting better" looks the same as "needs emergency baby heart surgery." All of us—me, Matt, my mother—are looking for some recognizable sign. The more time we spend with the boys at the hospital, the easier it will be to judge their progress.

But right now we are a captive audience for Chiara's performance.

"You sit dere," she tells Matt. "And you sit dere, Mama."

"Where do I get to sit?" Nonna asks. Chiara thinks for a moment and points to the hall, away from her makeshift stage in the dining room. Her message is clear. This show is for parents only.

"Oh, no! But Nonna wants to see you dance, too!" I say.

"Next time," our miniature prima donna replies. She turns to address her parents.

"Ladies and gentlemen! Da show is gonna start. Please turn off your cell phones!"

Chiara takes her place under two pictures taken in Reykjavik, the only two photographs I have of me dancing onstage. Snapshots of my ballet career never capture what I want to remember or how I felt in those moments. Instead they remind me of all the tiny imperfections. These two pictures from Iceland are the best ones that were taken of me and even those are full of faults. The knee that wasn't straight enough. The chin that was too high. The foot that could be pointed more.

Chiara turns on her music. She spins and leaps and poses. I'm amazed at my little daughter's proclivity for dance. She has a natural intuition for which way to spiral or turn or what part of a pose to hold. Of course, with her toddler proportions, she looks nothing like a dancer. She is pudgy and well-padded. Her round potbelly sticks out over her tutu. She has no self-awareness or self-consciousness. Her confidence is so pure, so sweet.

Halfway through the performance, she pulls Matt up from his chair to dance with her. She naturally arches when he hoists her over his head, perfectly supported by the palm of his hand between her tiny shoulder blades. With a little push, he throws his preschool diva high toward the ceiling and expertly catches her in a fish, a lift where the dancer's face is inches from the floor. Chiara squeals with delight. In her world, she is the ballerina and Daddy is her gallant cavalier.

Nonna has sneaked back into the dining room. She cheers wildly. "Brava, Chiara!"

This time Chiara does not send her away.

I haven't enrolled Chiara in any ballet classes, not even Mommy-and-Me dance classes at the ballet studio next door. Everything she has picked up has come from accompanying Matt to *Nutcracker* rehearsals or watching him onstage. We dance at home, too. From time to time she'll urge me to don my pointe shoes, old and perfectly broken in, and we'll dance together. About four months ago she found a bag of my old shoes while rummaging in the closet. Somewhere in another closet, I have a box of about twenty pairs of brand new Freed pointe shoes. Shoes I never got to wear because I didn't know my last year of dancing would be my last.

Chiara has only seen my old broken-in shoes. Some are peach-colored. Others are white or have been pancaked with makeup to match my skin color. All of them are smudged with rosin and dirt from the stage, war-torn but still beautiful. Each shoe has scribbled notes on its sole. There are frowny faces on shoes that pinched. Maybe the box of the shoe was lumpy or the stitches were uneven, or the satin wasn't pulled taut. There are smiley faces on the sturdy, solid shoes. The best ones—the shoes that gave extra support under the ball of the foot, flat and broad across the tip for good balance, didn't squeeze, didn't slip—got exclamation marks. I wasn't alone in my obsessions. One of my best friends gave names to each pair of her Freeds: George, Natalie, Major Suckage, Ice Cream.

There are other symbols on my shoes, clues to the career of a dancer. "C" is stamped into the leather of most of my shoes, for the cobbler who made them. There are other stamps: Bell, T, G. But C was my favorite. Some symbols are shorthand for ballets, such as a flower for a ballet that required shoes soft enough to jump in but hard enough to do light pointe work. Coming across the flower pair always turns my stomach a little. It's a reminder of the *pas de deux* and the overhead lift I was never able to master. After falling from Fausto's shoulders I'd had a hard time doing any kind of lift. Each rehearsal the director would change it a little, make it easier, his exasperation crystal clear as he'd stop the music and shake his head. Again.

"Oh-kaaay," he'd sigh. "Let's try this," until eventually it wasn't a lift at all but a simple do-si-do that even Chiara would be able to do. The flower drawn on the sole of those shoes always brings fresh regret. If only I'd been braver, maybe my contract would have been renewed. Maybe I would have danced longer.

I keep the pointe shoes around—even the new shoes that are

boxed away—because I have a hope that someday I'll get back in shape. Someday all this yoga and chiropractic work will heal me and I'll be able to dance again. Not at the professional level—after all, it's been ten years—but enough to be in the studio, leaping and turning and balancing on those shoes.

Chiara is both lost in the joy of her movements and relishing the attention of her rapt audience. Watching her dance makes me nostalgic. I can't imagine a childhood that does not involve ballet lessons. Ballet was everything—a way to get out of the Texas town that seemed so provincial and unsophisticated. A way to differentiate me from everyone else. Everything that I strived to do or finally achieved can be traced back to the discipline I acquired as a dancer. But then, there was also so much damage. Never being enough. Always falling short. How can I put my daughter into a world with so much self-loathing and negative reinforcement?

Chiara finishes her dance and takes several curtain calls. She runs offstage and comes back with imaginary flowers, which she then gifts to us. Perhaps she doesn't know that the dancer gets the flowers, not the crowd, that the gift she gives is the dance itself.

12

PAS DE DEUX

It's been five days since the surgeries. I walk into the NICU the same way I did yesterday and the day before and the day before that. Full makeup. Bright colors. My NICU shawl. Today it's my turquoise nursing tank top under a royal purple button-down shirt. The scent doll that I'll put in Michael's isolette peeks out from the top of my shirt. My mother and I sign in at the front desk. We flash our security bracelets. Just as we've done all of the twenty-six days that the boys have been here.

But today is different. Today nurses I have never seen before smile at us. Some of them greet me by name.

"Good morning, Mrs. Kovac!"

Others give me information after they grin and say hello.

"Michael and Wagner look great. The twins have really turned a corner."

My twins. How do they know my twins?

"They were so sick when they got here. Now look at them! They're so adorable."

"They weren't *sick*," my mother mutters to me. "Sick isn't the right word."

She washes her hands at the sink, soaping up to the elbows, and takes out a plastic disposable nail pick and cleans under her fingernails. My mother always goes the extra mile. She walks to the boys' room; I head to the family lounge to put our lunch in the fridge and snacks in our locker.

Another nurse. Another smile. Same words.

"Gosh, the twins look so great. Out of the woods." She shakes her head. "They were so sick."

Maybe "sick" is the hospital word for it, but I agree with my mother. The word "sick" is banana-slug green. My babies aren't green. They are blue and red. I don't think of them as being "sick" as much as just being tender, incomplete, the way a larva isn't a sick butterfly; it's a larva.

But what surprises me more than the word "sick" is the sudden recognition by the nurses. A light goes on in my head. We are a part of something here. We are not just customers. Until today I have been resisting true contact with them. There's polite small talk and of course our silly jokes, but mostly I just want them to hurry up and fix my kids. My impatience is much like the impatience I feel when our car is in the shop. I didn't know them; I assumed they didn't know me. But of course the nurses knew us. We have the tiniest and most fragile babies in the NICU right now. All the nurses are briefed on all the patients in their regular team meetings. In many cases they get to choose their assignments. Some nurses raise their hands to work with babies with precarious health concerns while others opt out.

All of a sudden I notice how many people are in the NICU. It's not just isolettes and heavy equipment. Some are doctors. I can tell because they wear white coats over business casual clothes. The nurses and technicians wear scrubs. Some are sky blue. Others are forest green or maroon. Some have patterns on them.

A nurse smiles at me as I walk down the hall to the boys' room.

According to her badge, her name is Kalpana. She has kittens on her hospital scrubs.

"The twins sure have turned a corner!" Kalpana says.

If I were back in college I could write a metaphor paper on this. "Turned a corner" means you were headed for one direction and now you are headed in a new direction—an outcome that was previously obscured. "Out of the woods" has a similar message. Previously you were lost "in the woods"—where it's dark and scary and no one knows what will happen. The twins aren't quite healthy enough for people to talk about the "light at the end of the tunnel." That'll be the next metaphor we'll hear.

The smiles of the nurses remind me of the grins of my ballet colleagues after they'd read the cast list and one of our gang had done the impossible—broken out into a role we thought none of us would get. To realize that the nurses knew more than we did about the boys' fragile health overshadows the good news that the boys are getting better. What else am I missing that is right in front of my eyes?

Another nurse I've never seen before strolls into the room. She makes some notes and looks at the dials. I look at her badge. Her name is Carlotta.

"Have you held your babies yet?" she asks, matter-of-factly, as though she's filling out a survey.

"They're not strong enough to be held," I tell her, matching her tone. It's been two weeks since I picked up Michael and he needed to be resuscitated and they just had surgery. I don't know how long it takes for micro preemies to be strong enough to be held.

"Nonsense!" says Carlotta. "I'll get some help."

She disappears and reappears with two other nurses, Dionne, who wears a bright Hawaiian print on her scrubs, and Grace, whom I recognize as one of the nurses who helped Wagner with his surgery.

"Michael just had his trophic feed so let's start with Wagner."

She hands me a hospital gown. "Put this on so it opens to the front," Carlotta instructs. "So you can hold him next to your skin. It's called 'Kangaroo care.'" Dionne pulls a curtain around me that I have never noticed before, a little privacy curtain that attaches to the ceiling to quarter off a small portion of the room. How is it that I've never noticed that this is here? I remove my shirt and nursing tank top and put on the gown.

An unspoken fear worms its way to the front of my consciousness—a thought I'd been pushing away. *If* they were in the fifty percent that didn't die and *if* they were in the remaining fifty percent that didn't have cerebral palsy or didn't go blind or deaf and *if* they were in the remaining half of that small number that didn't have cognitive disabilities, what kind of emotional damage would be incurred just because they were alone and uncuddled so much of the day? We spent as much time with them as we could, with a hand on the head and a hand on the soles of their feet, but was it enough?

Carlotta, Grace, and Dionne practically dance together to disconnect—then reconnect—various tubes and tape-affixed sensors. I am doubtful, hesitant. What if they forget to reconnect one of the tubes? What if the tubes don't reach? What if Wagner turns gray the way Michael did two weeks ago? There is so much equipment for such a little baby. They move Wagner out of his climate-controlled isolette and ease the two of us into a rocking chair. The hand-off is slow, deliberate, and unceremonious. All of a sudden I'm holding my baby. I'm holding Wagner for the first time.

I brace myself to feel nothing, anticipating an emotional detachment from my son. And if not emotional detachment, then I figure that cradling Wagner will mirror the hundreds (thousands?) of times that I've held Chiara. A hug where I feel that I am needed, where I feel that I am comforting her just because I am present. I assume that these are the only two possibilities.

Wagner's weight is like an anchor. He feels much heavier than two pounds. His warm little body feels like a hand on my heart. A part of me wants to stay on high alert; if something bad happens, I want to be ready. But the pull from my baby is stronger, as if we are swimming downwards to a place where seconds don't tick and machines don't beep.

Wagner snuggles into my skin, as if he knows me.

My baby knows me.

He nestles into my breast, making himself comfortable.

And I can tell: he's not mad or sad or damaged. He's happy and cuddly, as if we do this every day. As if it doesn't matter that he's twenty-six days old and has never been held before.

I cradle his head and he grasps the tip of my thumb, as if he knew it would be there to hold onto. The moons of his fingernails are pink. His hair is wavy. He has the best smell, a baby's smell. When he smacks his lips I can see tiny taste buds on his tongue.

Oh God. How I needed to hold my little baby. I am exhaling for the first time in twenty-six days. I feel relieved. Happy. So happy I can't even cry; I can only sigh deeply. When I do, Wagner melts into my chest. Alone in his isolette he might seem like a flickering candle, but with his head nestled on my breast he could be a generator for the sun.

13

WARMING UP

I have something to add to our locker in the family lounge: Matt's old flannel shirt. It's a standard-issue plaid from the days of grunge, like a grown-up security blanket. When I packed my bags to go to the hospital shortly before Chiara was born, I packed that shirt. I had visions of giving birth in it, wearing it when she was put on my chest so that she could smell both of her new parents at the same time. In reality I labored stark naked, moaning too loudly to be concerned about costume changes.

Finally the shirt has a purpose. The nurses want us to hold the babies skin-to-skin and if we keep the flannel shirt in our locker, it will always be clean, always smell like us. Maybe we can wear it when we hold the babies. But not today. Today Matt will wear a hospital gown, the way I did this morning when I held Wagner.

He is nervous. In the car on the way to the hospital, he makes excuses.

"It's okay. I don't need to hold them," he protests.

I don't tell him that he doesn't have a choice. Emma and Gordon, the nurses on the afternoon shift, will tell him that. He *has* to hold Michael. Now that the twins can be picked up, we have to hold them every day. Babies need to be held. Parents need to hold babies.

Besides, I restrained myself this morning from holding Michael. I wanted Matt to have his turn first. It will be part of our story.

"It'll be fine," I assure him.

Matt pulls into the parking garage and winds up to the third floor. He slides the car into the same spot he always parks in. During the day I have to park up on the fifth floor. All the spots are taken by 9 o'clock. But at night the garage is empty and we get to choose.

I am armed with milk for the fridge. Matt's flannel shirt is in a decorative bag. The scent doll is in my shirt. I'll put it in Wagner's isolette tonight and swap it out for the blue one with the plaid star that I put there a few days ago. I wonder if I'll be able to smell Wagner on the scent doll the way I could smell him on my skin this afternoon.

At the front desk on the ground floor there is a line. Everyone who comes in after 8:30 p.m. has to sign in. Sometimes they recognize us and wave us through. Maybe they recognize my olive green shawl. Maybe it's the scent doll peeking out of my shirt. Maybe it's the bracelets we have on our wrists. But today we have to wait in line like everybody else. It's a different security guard, one I haven't met before. I look at his nametag and snap a mental picture of his face: Oscar. Next time I'll greet him by name.

We sign in. Matt is jittery, too jittery to make jokes even. I know I am making him do something he doesn't want to do.

We have our smiles ready for the security guard on the NICU floor.

"Hi, Justine!" I say brightly. She smiles and hands us a pen to sign in again.

"Say hello to your mother for me," she says. I feel like a celebrity.

"We're going to hold babies tonight," I say confidently. I don't have to look at Matt. I know that he's clenching his jaw, wishing I hadn't said anything.

We pass the threshold into the NICU. It's as if everyone is an old friend now.

"Hi, Derek! Hi, Nisha!" There's a third person at the desk tonight. He must be new. He's methodically wiping each page of a plastic notebook with antibacterial wipes. The new guy is always the one on binder detail. I don't know why they need to wipe down the notebooks, but I guess you can't be too careful. Or maybe it just reinforces how sterilized everything needs to be.

I peek down at the flannel shirt in the bag. It feels dirty, having come into this sanitized space, even though it is freshly washed. But I can't be sure: did I let it rest on the arm of the couch or the edge of our bed? Maybe it's not clean enough. I lock the bag and shirt in Locker 25. I know I'll take it back home with me and wash it again.

"Are you ready?" asks Gordon.

Matt looks startled, as if he has just been handed a pop quiz written in a foreign language.

If we weren't in the NICU, Gordon might pat Matt on the back. But here no one touches anyone; they'd just have to wash their hands again. Instead Gordon corners Matt, herding him toward the rear of the room like a sheepdog.

Matt pumps some hand sanitizer into his palm, even though we have both just washed our hands two minutes ago.

I am so excited. I want him to have this moment to cherish.

"The fathers never want to hold the babies. Kangaroo care makes them nervous," Wagner's nurse Emma had said to me earlier.

Matt would be different, I thought. I had an entire Facebook album of pictures of Matt holding Chiara. In his arms, on his head. Even a picture of her balancing on the palm of his hand when she was just six months old. It was part of their Father-Daughter Circus Act, the main event after the Father-Daughter Dance Party. They also had a Father-Daughter Magic Trick. This is not a guy who's afraid to hold his kids.

"We have to make them," Gordon said. "But don't worry; we're professionals."

"It's so important," Emma added. "Kangaroo care helps the babies stay warm. They breathe better when their parents are holding them and sleep better afterwards."

The medical benefits were fantastic, but I wanted Matt to hold his son so he could feel what I'd felt earlier today. I hadn't realized how badly I needed to hold my little boys. I had blocked it out of mind after Michael had needed to be resuscitated. If they weren't healthy enough yet, why dwell on it? But now that I had held Wagner, an ache had been soothed. Kangaroo care wouldn't just comfort the babies; it would comfort us too.

"You're ready," Gordon tells Matt, who stands very stiffly, pretending he's not squirming inside.

"Are you sure it's okay?" Matt says, but it feels like he's really saying, "I don't think I can do this."

He is cornered in the back of the boys' room. If he could escape, I'm certain he would make some excuse and leave. But there is too much equipment between him and the wide sliding-glass door that leads from the boys' room into the hallway. There are two ventilators, two monitors, two isolettes, two portable nursing carts. There is a rocking chair and a breast pump on a wheeled stand, and three other adults who could hold him down. It feels like an intervention.

Matt shifts his weight from foot to foot. He puts his hands out in front of him as if to push away something very heavy.

"I don't want to hurt them," he stutters.

"We do this all the time," Emma says reassuringly, but I think she's saying, "You have no choice." She presses her hand onto Matt's shoulder and he obediently sits down into a peach-colored vinyl rocking chair, the same one I sat in when I held Wagner earlier today. I put a hand on his other shoulder. Not for comfort, but to keep him there.

Michael's isolette has side flaps that open upwards, like a garage door. The tubes won't stretch from the ventilator through the isolette to the rocking chair so Gordon unplugs them. There is no air going into Michael's lungs at this moment, at least not from the NICU equipment. Matt isn't breathing, either. Gordon's hands move deliberately, much slower than they need to move. Matt looks scared. C'mon, I think to him, the boys can do this now. It's safe, only three seconds while Gordon reconnects the breathing tube.

The heart monitor is next. It's just a sensor. A sticker, really, and the alarm beeps when Gordon peels it off Michael's belly. He snakes it back through a hole at the front of Michael's isolette and reattaches the sensor. Finally he detaches the feeding tube, the most inconsequential of the tubes, at least right now.

"Please," Matt begs. "You don't have to go through all this work for me."

Don't be afraid, I think. You balanced Chiara on your hand because you knew she'd be safe. If you could do that, you can do this.

Emma puts Michael in his father's arms. Matt holds him gingerly, as if he is a grenade. He doesn't look at him. He doesn't see what I saw in his brother when I held him earlier today. He doesn't see the whorls of hair, blond and wet. He doesn't see the puckered skin on Michael's cheeks where the tape holds the breathing tube in place. His eyes are glued to the monitor. He is checking Michael's numbers: 87...86...85. He knows that when it gets down to 83, the alarm will sound. If it gets lower than that he knows that Emma and Gordon will take the baby away, which will actually make him feel better. At least then Michael will be safe inside his isolette.

Emma rotates the monitor so he can't read it. She puts a hand on his shoulder guiding him as he leans back against the rocking chair. She puts her other hand on the back of his, the one that holds Michael, gently but firmly, as if there is a Velcro strip between father and son and she is trying to make them stick together. Michael's entire back fits in the palm of Matt's hand.

Matt looks up helplessly, not at Emma, but at the side of the monitor. He starts to protest, but the words are lost in his throat. Finally, he exhales and Michael sinks into his chest. They stay like that for six, maybe seven minutes. Father and son together for the first time.

Matt never closes his eyes.

14

INTERMISSION

We take such pains to give Chiara all of our attention when we're home. I never leave for the hospital before I drop her off at daycare and Matt and I never go to the NICU at night until she's asleep. Nonetheless, she screams, "MAMA! DON'T LEAVE ME!" every time I take a shower. Did the ten days that I spent in the hospital from Christmas through New Year's feel like abandonment? Or can she tell that my attention is divided when we're at home? Either way, we need to have some special mother-daughter time together.

A Russian ballet company is performing in Marin County north of San Francisco at a theater where Matt has often danced the *Nutcracker*. They are here for one night. They'll be dancing *Coppélia*. The timing is auspicious: the performance falls on the eve of Chiara's third birthday. It feels like the perfect opportunity for us to spend some time together.

She's sat through countless rehearsals of Matt's and several two-hour performances. I think she can handle this full-length ballet. I'm less confident about my own ability to sit through the performance. I haven't been to a ballet, other than to watch Matt dance, in years. I can't stand to watch all those other dancers—some better than I had been, others not as good, but all of them younger and healthier. And nearly every ballet reminds me of the backstage politics or some slight I'd endured while dancing. I feel fresh humiliations as I relive a stumble and renewed indignation when I remember the roles I thought I'd deserved but didn't get to dance. Although really there's no winning. I'd probably rather watch a ballet that reminds me of failure than one that reminds me of success. The last thing I want to do is watch someone else dance something that I cherish. I don't want visions of another dancer to record over my own memories.

When I tell my mother that I've purchased tickets on the aisle in case we need to beat a hasty retreat, she assumes it's for Chiara's sake. Really, it's for mine.

I know my little girl will get the most out of the ballet if she knows the story or has heard some of the music beforehand so we spend a week watching the ballet on YouTube. It's also an opportunity for me to hear music I haven't heard in over seventeen years. Listening to music is such a visceral experience for a dancer. When I hear the lullaby of Stravinsky's *Firebird*, my heart reverberates through my muscles. Dancing the lead in that ballet was one of my grand slams. The mazurka from *Coppélia*, on the other hand, just reminds me of the sting I'd felt dancing in the corps in Iceland under the director's scowl and Eva Evdokimiva's criticism.

As Chiara nestles up to my laptop, I try to explain the plot. It's harder than I thought it would be.

"That's Swanhilda. She's the main dancer."

I don't remember who told me that I hadn't been cast as Swanhilda. Eva Evdokimiva gave herself the role in the first cast, of course, and picked a young seventeen-year-old that she'd found in New York as second cast. Third cast went to the Icelandic dancer with the most seniority. I might have found this out looking at the cast list, long after everyone else had crowded in front of the bulletin board. Most likely I heard the news from the aging ballet master who'd brought me from El Paso to Reykjavik. He was also the one trying to start a rumor that Eva and the young seventeen-year-old girl were having a lesbian affair. The rumor didn't take.

I don't remember if I was invited to understudy as a consolation prize or if I took it upon myself in an attempt to prove my worth. I do remember sulking my way through rehearsals, slinking in the back of the studio, learning not only Swanhilda's many solo variations but every role in the ballet, even the male ones. Whenever someone was injured, I'd jump in and do their part. In an American ballet company I would have been one of several dancers lingering in the back, trying to show her worth by learning other parts. But in Iceland I was the only one who took this initiative. I loved the way it made me stand out. *Janine knows* that *part, too!*

So when Chiara and I watch Swanhilda dance with her fiancé Franz, I remember not only her steps but his as well.

I describe the pantomime to Chiara. "See what Swanhilda is doing with her hands?"

Swanhilda points to Dr. Coppelius' house and pounds her fist. All the villagers nod and pound their fists.

"She's saying, 'That old man works very hard.'"

Swanhilda points to Dr. Coppelius' house and makes stiff doll motions. The villagers make stiff doll motions, too.

"Now she's saying, 'That old man makes dolls.'"

I had learned the choreography for Dr. Coppelius as well. The ballet master had been the obvious choice to dance the role, but he was too vain to don the character of a creepy old man and refused to learn the steps. A renowned Icelandic thespian had been recruited to perform the part, but he wasn't available for daily rehearsals. The other male dancers also refused to learn the role. Like the ballet master, they were afraid that they'd be downgraded as glorified mimes instead of recognized for the dancers they were.

So I rehearsed the part. It was the one role where I could capture everyone's attention. The whole studio would stop to watch what I would do next. I'd play with the timing of visual jokes to milk the laughs. Since all of the cues for Act II are taken from Dr. Coppelius, I knew I was also being helpful while annoying the director at the same time. She had no choice but to let me rehearse the part that no one else wanted to dance. It felt like the best kind of revenge. I don't know if this was before or after the director started courting the dancer she'd cast as Franz, but I know it was before she found out that he spent most of his nights at my place.

On YouTube, the ballerina who dances Swanhilda points to Dr. Coppelius' house a third time, then points to her head, circling her finger to make the universal sign for "crazy." The villagers laugh and copy her.

"Now what she say?" Chiara asks.

"She says, 'That old man is *crazy*.'"

Chiara gasps. At her Berkeley preschool "crazy" is a bad word.

"Why?"

"Well, because he makes life-size dolls and he thinks his dolls can come to life."

Dr. Coppelius pretends Coppélia is his daughter instead of a doll. Franz thinks Coppélia is a pretty girl who likes him. When Swanhilda discovers the truth about Coppélia, who is making mechanical advances toward her fiancé, she dresses in the doll's clothes. And now both Franz and Dr. Coppelius think that Swanhilda is Coppélia. Meanwhile, the audience has kept everything straight and is still entertained.

Unfortunately, it's a little harder to describe to a three-year-old. Chiara can barely grasp that the huge toy onstage is actually a motionless dancer. And I have completely underestimated how hard it is to explain the finer points of coquetry—or even the more obvious ones, for that matter.

"Well, you see, Franz and Swanhilda were engaged to be married until she caught him blowing kisses to a doll and called off the engagement. Which is, of course, why she's dressing up in the doll's clothes and destroying Dr. Coppelius' workshop."

Particularly confusing is the part where Dr. Coppelius drugs Franz so that he can steal his soul and give it to the doll. Who of course isn't a doll but a ballet dancer pretending to be a doll who has come to life and throws stuff at the scenery.

Chiara is aghast. "She made a big messes! Dat not nice!" She doesn't understand the subtleties of a jealous girlfriend playing hard to get and a creepy old man who roofies the male lead, but she does get that it's not cool to destroy things.

I am equally horrified. Apparently during my career, I had been too caught up in learning as many steps as possible to notice that this is a really silly ballet, the opposite of higher culture. I might as well be exposing my daughter to episodes of *Jersey Shore*.

By the time the performance rolls around on Friday night I'm questioning my decision to go to the ballet at all. Everything about this mother-daughter evening spells disaster. The theater is forty-five minutes away. The show doesn't even start until Chiara's bedtime. And of course it's raining. Drive time plus performance duration means that there will be over four hours between pumping so I'll need to take a hand pump with me. If working women can pump in their offices at their jobs, I can pump in a bathroom stall, right?

Chiara has insisted on wearing her "fancy dress," a sapphire blue velvet dress with a layer of tulle underneath and her hair in a bun. She is by far the smallest audience member, and some ticket-holders glare at us, as if to say, "That child isn't going to make noise, is she?"

Others comment on her outfit. "Are you a dancer?" they coo.

"Sometimes," she answers shyly.

Our seats are on the aisle, as planned. In the row in front of us sits a white-haired couple. Judging from her cane and his agility, it looks like a son accompanying his elderly mother to the ballet. It's hard to say who is more excited, his mother or my daughter.

When the lights dim and the overture begins to play, the old woman's head bobs in time with the music and her hand waves back and forth as if she is conducting the orchestra.

"We aren't going to have a sing-along now, are we?" the man pre-emptively reprimands his mother. She doesn't answer, hands clasped at her chest, as if this evening is better than Christmas morning. Her son mutters something to her but she doesn't stop.

I fantasize that she was once a dancer, too. That like me, she danced in this ballet, but obviously it holds better memories for her. Will I one day be like this old woman, escorted by one of my children to the ballet so I can relive my past life?

When the curtain opens on Swanhilda and she tiptoes out on stage, the music, sweet and twinkly, makes me grit my teeth. The gentle opening solo takes me right back to Reykjavik. The second season, when we reprised *Coppélia*, I was sure that I'd get to dance at least one performance as Swanhilda. The young seventeen-year-old had gone back to New York; Eva Evdokimiva was back in London. It should have been my role. But when I went to check the casting list, my name wasn't there at all. Not for the principal roles. Not for the soloist roles. Not even for the corps de ballet roles I'd danced the year before.

"Well, someone will get injured. You can dance for them when they're out since you know all the parts, anyway," the director smirked when I met with her in her office. By this time she knew I was the reason Franz had denied her advances. She was clearly enjoying this.

She was right—several dancers injured themselves and I ended up dancing a number of roles. But I was always thrust in at the last min-ute. Another form of retaliation. I left the company shortly after that.

For the next two acts I count up all the dancers' transgressions.

This one is out of line, that one was early on her music. I tally up bent knees and sickled feet. Chiara is mesmerized by the ballet, but it's put me in a foul mood.

Meanwhile, my breasts are engorged and starting to leak. During intermission I try to pump in the bathroom. The effort lasts a whole seven seconds. What was I thinking? There's no place to sit. No place for a three-year-old to wait. There's certainly no place to put sterilized breast pump equipment. Even if I had been successful, where would I have put the milk? In my purse?

At the end of the second act, I'm ready to go.

"Ballet is over, sweetie! Time to go home!" I tell Chiara.

"We hafta stay for da wedding!"

Damn. I should have known she'd remember that the ballet had a wedding.

"But it's late, honey."

"Just one more dance?" she bargains and I concede.

It's very late, past her bedtime, and she crawls into my lap as the third act starts. From time to time she whispers, "Now what happen?"

I can't remember the last time I just held her on my lap. I can feel her chest rise and fall as she breathes and it occurs to me that I never feel the boys breathe when I hold them. Are they just too small or is it because they are too weak to breathe deeply? By contrast my daughter feels so strong, so heavy, so full of life.

There's an overture. A march. And then the first *divertissements:* the Dance of the Hours, one of the corps roles I'd danced. Chiara and I didn't watch this part in the YouTube videos. I haven't heard this music in seventeen years. The pale lavender music starts slowly, like a flower blossoming, and as it progresses, I feel a surge of joy.

Wow, I think, caught off guard. I must have really enjoyed dancing this.

First comes the feeling, then the memory. I *did* enjoy this dance. I loved how it started delicate and sparkly and then grew into a grand waltz with big jumps before returning to delicate steps again. I loved how light and full my skirt was and how each *grand jeté* felt like a surprise, as if the music lifted me instead of the choreography. It's like comfort food. Better. It feels like coming home.

Now I remember—that's why I stayed in Iceland through the end of that first year after it became apparent that the director didn't like me and that Icelandic dancers would always be favored over foreigners. It didn't matter to me that it wasn't a technical part or a glorified role. It didn't matter that there wasn't anyone in the audience who had come to see me dance. It didn't even matter that it wasn't my role to start with. Because there was joy inside and it wanted to come out. This is why we dance. This is why I want my daughter to see dance.

After the dancers bow and exit gracefully, Chiara whispers, "Now we can go."

I kiss the top of her head and we make our own graceful exit back to the car.

15

THEMES AND VARIATIONS

Now that we can hold the boys, our visits to the NICU have a purpose. We have a log and a schedule and between Matt, Nonna, and me, each baby is held for almost an hour twice a day. Every time the boys are moved from the isolette to the rocking chair, the transition goes a little more smoothly. Matt is a true convert now and sometimes even returns to the NICU during the night shift for another round of Kangaroo care. Holding the boys makes us feel like parents. But it also feels like nourishment—not just for them, but for us, too. We are not just bystanders in the NICU anymore.

Just when it feels like we're making real progress, the day nurse Grace delivers some bad news.

"So, Wagner had a hard night last night." She says this softly, slowly, as if there might be more grave news.

I look at Wagner's chart. There are clusters of red circles at various times from the late evening through the night and again this morning.

"These aren't his usual de-sats," she explains. "These episodes were apneic."

Apneic. Not breathing.

"Everything's fine now. His numbers are good."

I look at the monitor. Breaths per minute, oxygen-saturation rate, PEEPs, PAPs, PIPs, all good. I still can't remember what the acronyms stand for. To me they are all just green bubbles in my head. But I do know their corresponding normal ranges and everything looks normal.

"We have new doctor's orders. Limit holding to once a day, no more than an hour."

I can't hold my babies? How could having your mama hold you possibly be dangerous? That can't be the problem. After all, nobody was holding Wagner at night around his cluster of episodes.

"We want you to hold them, but if they're having problems . . ." she trails off. "Sometimes it's...we just have to see how they handle it."

Michael's fine. Same kind of monitor. Same kind of respirator. Same kind of numbers. Different night. I take his temperature. I give him his pacifier. I change his diaper and put it on the tray so it can be weighed. I change the oxygen sensor from his foot to his wrist. His wrist is big enough now.

"Hey! The PICC line is out!" I exclaim. "PICC" is another green bubble to me. I just know that it's something the boys needed after surgery. Something that shouldn't stay in too long and brings with it the risk of infection after it comes out.

"Yes, they took it out last night. The boys are up on their feedings, down on the TPN. They don't need their IVs anymore."

"So maybe that's why Wagner had a bad night?"

"Could be." Her voice trails up as she shrugs. "We'll just have to wait and see." Her voice is reassuring but firm and clear. I will not be able to hold Wagner today, and since Michael has just completed his feeding I won't be able to hold him, either. It's too hard for Michael to digest his food when he's upright.

Grace leaves with Michael's diaper. After she weighs it, she'll record the result in his file.

I adjust Michael's pacifier again, wondering if I could persuade Grace to let me hold Wagner before I have to pick up Chiara from daycare. Not for a whole hour, just a little bit. Twenty minutes. Or even ten minutes. A high-pitched alarm breaks my train of thought. It's a de-sat. Wagner's monitor flashes and I see the readings pop up on the screen. Forty-eight.

Forty-eight.

Wagner has dropped from a safe stage somewhere between eighty and ninety-seven, triggered the alarm, and in two seconds he's now at forty-eight. In all of their daily de-sats, I've never seen it drop so low so quickly. The room is dark. Grace is still weighing Michael's diaper. I'm alone with the twins.

A second later, Xian, the nurse from the room next to us, rushes in. Because I'm at Michael's isolette, she thinks the problem is with him. I nod toward Wagner and I tell her, "He's at forty-eight."

Grace returns. She is calm. Too calm?

I finish with Michael. I should be panicking but instead my focus narrows, as if I am getting ready to dance on a slippery stage. I don't have time to panic. I just have to take it one step at a time. Focus in. Don't waver.

More flashing numbers: 43. 38. 33.

"He's at nine," Grace says, reading the monitor. "Breaths. He's at nine breaths. Twenty-five. He's back up to 25."

"Give him some more oxygen," Xian tells her. "I upped his oxygen but give him some more."

"Come on, Wagner. Breathe, honey, you've got to breathe," Grace says.

I'm not breathing, either.

"Tap him on his back."

38. 44. 55. 56. 57.

"Give him a little more oxygen."

55.

"Breathe, honey. Come, on." Grace whispers to Wagner as she taps him on his back.

Oh, please, breathe. Please breathe.

67. 73. 78. 85.

The monitor stops flashing.

The nurses discuss whether the episode was apnea or not. His heart rate only dropped to 119. Technically, an apneic episode would have had a heart rate of 90s or lower. But given the cluster of apneas last night, they'll count it as one.

The monitor beeps again.

97. 98. 99. 100.

He's stabilized. The nurses and I look at each other and sigh with relief. Grace lowers Wagner's oxygen. If my mother were here, she'd ask, "What happened? Are you sure he's okay now? Will it happen again?" But to me, we are still onstage, dancing in the moment. Don't look forward. Don't look back. Stay right here and right now, everything is fine.

Later that afternoon I return to the hospital with Matt.

Emma, the boys' afternoon nurse, is in conversation with the doctor.

"I think we should do some tests. There could be an infection from taking the PICC line out. All it takes is one little germ," she says.

The doctor agrees, shrugging, "Sure. You never know."

They take a blood-gas reading, looking for clues as to what might be causing this fluctuation in Wagner's breathing. The results come back normal. They snap an X-ray. The lungs look cloudy but nothing too different from yesterday's X-ray.

The next step is to take blood—some for tests, some for a culture. But Wagner's arm spasms. They can't get the needle in. Sofia is called in to try. Another spasm. Three nurses try another limb with a tourniquet this time. Emma holds Wagner's arm while Blanca pokes it. Gordon stands by with a sterilized strip of paper.

Matt and I watch Wagner's arm, strangely listless. It doesn't even react to the needle prick. Usually we'd see it contract. Wagner should flinch. His reflexes should involuntarily react but it's as if he is comatose. Too cautious to pace, we stand there, arms crossed, brows furrowed, lips tense.

Finally, Sofia finds a vein. The blood goes from Wagner's ankle to a thin tube to a strip of paper.

Matt clears his throat. "Uh, why was his arm like that?"

"Sucrose," Gordon says. "We put a drop of sucrose on the tongue. For infants it acts like a pain killer."

Matt and I both sigh, relieved. Sucrose. So natural and simple, providing comfort rather than being a symptom of grave sickness. Matt looks at me with a tight grin. His eyes are not smiling. He has no joke at the ready. I wonder if he is thinking what I am thinking, that we can't tell the difference between a medical remedy and an emergency.

The results come back picture perfect. No infection.

After we put Chiara to bed, we leave her with my mom and go back to the hospital one more time. Wagner's saturation rate is high and his oxygen percentage rate is low, both of which are very good.

"We still have to wait for the results of the blood culture, but it looks like we'll never know what caused this cluster of apneas," Steph the night nurse says. "Sometimes that's just what preemies do."

I don't know what this means. If I will be able to hold Wagner tomorrow or not again until next week. Or if Wagner will be fine but Michael will be the one with an unexplainable crisis.

In my ballet career I could never look too far down the road. I could dream about being a principal dancer for San Francisco Ballet, but I couldn't imagine the road that would take me there. My visibility into the future was usually just the next performance or the current season. I thought that I wasn't as successful as I wanted to be because I didn't plan well enough.

Now, that lack of visibility feels like a coping device. I can picture the boys as grown men with college diplomas or tuxedos on their wedding day, but I can't picture how we'll get from today to tomorrow. I can't see the boys as babies in a crib in our home or as toddlers who will push us to baby-proof the staircase. The only picture I can hold in my brain is Wagner's limp arm, anesthetized by sugar beets.

16

DIVERTISSMENTS

On the day of the boys' two-month vaccinations I get a newsletter from a pregnancy website. According to them, my babies are still fetuses.

"At thirty-three weeks pregnant," the email reads, "you are probably thinking about your baby's delivery. If you haven't already, you need to start preparing to go to the hospital at any moment. Even though your due date is seven weeks away, you want to be prepared for any pregnancy complications that may occur, such as premature labor."

Meanwhile, mybaby.com makes other assumptions. In its emails I'm told that my two-month-old baby likes to look at colors and patterns. Chiara was that kind of baby—reaching for toys dangled in front of her. But the two-month-old babies I have now are still hooked up to breathing machines and are still fed through a tube in the nose.

Today we have another meeting with the neonatologist, the nurse manager, and the social worker. They'll talk to us about the boys' progress and milestones. Last time we talked about pediatricians and the sort of doctor who would understand the special needs that preemies might have. This time I don't know what's on their agenda, but I know what's on ours. According to the Parent

Care Chart the NICU has given us, "recreational breastfeeding" was supposed to start three weeks ago.

The trouble is, neither Matt nor I know what "recreational breastfeeding" is. We're afraid to ask. We're worried that it might mean something between the parents rather than something for the babies. It's taken us three weeks to work up the nerve to bring it up because we don't want our fears confirmed. I know that when a mother's milk ducts are a little plugged, it's not uncommon to ask for the assistance of someone who has a stronger musculature for sucking and how that someone often comes in the form of a polite and willing partner. But that seems more "utilitarian" than "recreational." "Recreational" for me brings up images of lemonade and ping-pong and possibly even other people. Matt and I want to be good students but we are also prudent folk. On the other hand this *is* Berkeley. Who knows what's expected of us.

"You ask."

"No, *you* ask."

The meeting progresses nicely. The boys are nearly three pounds apiece, which seems enormous to us. They are almost ready to go in an open crib, which means that they'll come out of their little Plexiglas boxes into tiny but normal-looking cribs. And since our hospital puts twins together, our boys won't be alone anymore; they'll be swaddled up next to each other. It's a new chapter. We are invited to bring a mobile from home if we have one. We can even start to dress them in baby clothes.

"The boys are doing so well," the doctor informs us. "Do you have any questions? Anything we haven't covered?"

I can feel Matt nudging me with his eyes.

I clear my throat and try to sound casual.

"Yeah. So, uh. I'm reading our Parent Care Chart and I noticed there's some stuff we haven't started yet."

I unfold our care chart and brush my hand over *Week 31: Recreational Breastfeeding.*

"Oh, yes," the doctor nods. "Well, you see, it's really hard for babies of this gestation to suck, swallow, *and* breathe. It involves a lot of coordination. So the recreational breastfeeding is like an intermediate step."

"Ah," Matt nods even though this explanation doesn't explain anything. He pauses. "So that means we…uh…what do we have to do?"

The nurse manager cocks her head, trying to understand and when she does, she blushes. "Nothing! It's not for you. It's for the babies. It just means they try to nurse without really feeding."

Now we're the ones who look like sexual deviants, like we're that kinky Berkeley couple anxious to make the most out of my milk ducts. We spurt and sputter. "Good! Yes. Whew. We didn't want…I mean, we didn't know…But of course we want do whatever we need to do."

Matt is torn. He wants the staff to know that he is the sort of husband who is eager and willing to go above and beyond but he doesn't want them to think he is too eager and willing.

"Good." Matt smacks his thigh and shuts his notebook. "So, uh. We'll get started on that today." He looks at me. "I mean, you'll get started on that right away. I'll just watch. Or uh, not watch. I'll just, uh. Do whatever you need me to do."

That night, after we read books to Chiara and tuck her into bed, Matt and I drive to the hospital. Our routine feels like a choreographed dance. Downstairs we sign in at the security desk. Upstairs we get dressed so that we can hold the twins skin-to-skin. Me in my olive green shawl and Matt in his plaid button-down flannel. We secure our bags in our locker in the family lounge. We soap up for thirty seconds and wash under our fingernails. We bring two rocking chairs to Room 1. By now we are experts at taking our boys out of their isolettes. Tomorrow I'll bring some of the baby clothes that I sorted back in December before I was admitted to the hospital. An apple red onesie for Michael and a royal blue one for Wagner. But for tonight we'll just hold the boys in their diapers.

They still look so tiny, so different from normal newborns. They spend almost all their time sleeping, not reacting. Sometimes we find Michael with an arm over his head as if the light is too bright for him or catch Wagner with a hand down his diaper. But they look like someone has posed them.

I can't remember what Chiara was like as a two-month-old, but I know it was more than this. She made eye contact and copied our facial expressions. She stuck her tongue out when we did and mimicked our wide smiles. It seems as if her personality was always present, as if she was born loving ruffles and sequins. In my memory she has always wiggled from side to side in a happy shimmy when eating favorite foods. She has always known how to be the center of attention.

The boys, on the other hand, are oblivious to us. They don't even have gassy smiles that could falsely be attributed to contentment. It's as if they are still undercooked and need more time. I'm desperate for any indication that my sons are actually little human beings with desires and intentions. But I still only see the colors. Blue for the sound sleeper that Wagner is and red for Michael's jerky motions.

After Matt and I record the boys' temperatures, change their diapers, and remove and replace their oxygen-saturation cuffs, we each take a twin. I have Michael; Matt holds Wagner. We sit in our respective vinyl chairs on opposite sides of the room.

If we both cock our heads to the side, we can see each other through the machines and wires. From time to time we lock eyes. It's dim at night but I can still see the contentment in Matt's face, as if he is purring. Then—surprise. His eyes widen and his muscles tense. Wagner has started to root. He's inching his way toward Matt's nipple, licking his lips, so intent on his goal that he doesn't even notice the hairy chest.

It's the kind of thing a *baby* would do. A baby who can smell. A baby with instincts that tell him that food is nearby. A baby with goals.

"Recreational breastfeeding!" I exclaim in a loud whisper.

Matt's grin is broad. "Buddy," he says to his son. "You are going to be so disappointed."

I rock forward slightly in my chair and look down at the baby on my own chest. The sides of Michael's skull are flat from the hours spent lying on his belly with his head turned to the side. The nurses call it "toaster head" because it has the shape of an old-fashioned toaster, although they're not supposed call it toaster head in front of the parents.

Michael yawns and this reflex also looks so much like that of a real baby it's startling. The nurses have promised me that the boys won't go to kindergarten with toaster heads. Kindergarten feels so far away. I can't imagine that they will ever be bigger than they are now—just over three pounds.

When it's time to go, I carefully put Michael back into his isolette as Matt puts Wagner into his. They have fewer tubes now and we don't need as much help holding them.

Michael lies on his back. His eyes squeeze shut even tighter. He opens his mouth and waves his arms. Tiny squeaks come out. I have never heard him cry before. I didn't think he could.

My baby is crying.

It's so much softer than Chiara's cries when she was two months old. And yet, it's the same cry. Mama, don't leave me. Hold me again.

I should feel a pang that makes me want to pick him back up and comfort him. But I'm so happy to hear him complain, and if I pick him up it will be over too quickly. He'll stop talking to me. I stand there, soaking up his tiny squawks, committing them to memory with colors, cries that swirl in luscious streaks of indigo and scarlet.

17

LEAVING THE
THEATER

The boys are going home soon—probably within the next two weeks. If this had been a typical pregnancy, I'd be eight and half months pregnant right now and ready to deliver healthy spring babies. Instead the twins are twelve weeks old. Wagner just hit six pounds and Michael is not far behind at five pounds and thirteen ounces.

We have spent the last ten days in Room 22, which is tucked away in the back of the NICU. I can't help but relish the thought: there is light at the end of the tunnel. It's hard to believe that when the boys were born nearly three months ago, each one had a nurse whose only job was to stand in front of the isolette, adjusting dials, making sure that her patient continued to breathe and that his heart continued to beat. They couldn't even leave to go to the bathroom or take a phone call.

In Room 22 the boys are together in an open crib. No more iso-lettes. They are swaddled in blankets we brought from home, dressed in preemie clothes that almost fit. We brought Chiara's old crib mobile, the one that mechanically beeps thirty-two measures from Bee-thoven, then Bach, then Mozart while oddly shaped animals in contrasting colors of tangerine, jade, and indigo slowly dance around. The mobile agitated Chiara; she hated it. But the boys find it soothing. We know because as soon as we turn it on, the oxygen-saturation numbers on the monitor rise.

Being healthy enough to think about the boys leaving the NICU also means that they are healthy enough to share a room with another baby. We get a new one every couple of days, and they are usually term babies that are kept overnight as a precaution.

Our current roommate is Alexander, a late preemie born at four pounds. I don't know the details, but I do know that he has been here for three weeks. Alexander's mother Anita always brings six bottles of breast milk when she visits. She has more milk than Alexander could ever drink, which for some reason makes her feel guilty. As if overcompensating with a surplus of nutrition means that she has been negligent in some other area. Or perhaps it's the other way around— Anita had to choose between taking maternity leave three weeks ago when Alexander was born or taking it when he comes home from the hospital. She chose to take it later, which means she can only visit for an hour or so each night after work.

I usually don't talk to the other parents. I'm never sure what they might be going through and I don't know how to engage in conversation. I know I don't want to talk about our near-death experiences. I assume the other parents don't either. But now that we'll be going home soon, Matt and I have taken the mandatory discharge class, the one that teaches us infant CPR and gives information about SIDS. That's how I know that Anita went back to work four days after Alexander was born. We're in the same class.

Today we are both in Room 22. We nod our hellos but don't talk to each other.

When Anita takes Alexander out of his crib she coos in a high-pitched sing-songy voice.

"How's my baby today? So biiiiiig!!! Oh, you're so big!"

Like the boys, Alexander is too weak to nurse, but unlike them, he has no trouble drinking from a bottle. When Anita feeds him, she doesn't have to angle the bottle and baby away from her to minimize choking, the way I do. Our boys need forty-five minutes just to drink six ounces. Alexander drinks his in half that time.

Anita cradles her son in her lap. She rocks him as she feeds him and sings little lullabies.

I used to sing to Chiara when she was a baby. Matt made up a song, "Chiara the Baby Likes Cheese; She Really, Really Likes Cheese" sung to the tune of "Volare." We'd sing it all the time. But I never sing to the twins. I don't rock them, either. I guess I still think of them as micro preemies who get overstimulated from the slightest stroke.

While Anita hums to Alexander, I turn my attention to paperwork. We have handouts from the discharge class, a quiz I have to turn in to prove we're ready.

How many breaths to chest pumps for infant CPR?

What vitamins will your baby need when he goes home?

What do you do when the pharmacy changes the dose of your iron supplement?

What's the difference between your baby's chronological age and her adjusted age?

Matt and I know all the answers. There are two breaths to thirty chest pumps for infant CPR. Our babies will need Polyvisol vitamins added to their formula, and if we have questions about their iron supplements we can check the concentration. Adjusted age is basically just counting from when our twins should have been born instead of when they *were* born. This is especially important because they were born so early. In fact, even though chronologically they are almost three months old now, we are still counting in gestational weeks. According to the nurses, our boys are thirty-eight weeks' gestation, not twelve weeks old.

Right now it's easy to think of them as newborn babies, but months from now, when they are seven months old and still not sitting up, we'll need to remind ourselves that they are actually four months old. They'll have their first birthday next December, but as far as the nurses are concerned, Michael and Wagner won't be a year old until three and a half months later on April 10th. Most babies catch up by their second or third birthday and we are already enrolled in early intervention therapy to monitor our progress once we leave the NICU.

Anita kisses the top of Alexander's head and it occurs to me that maybe I know all the right answers for our discharge quiz, but I've spent more time trying to act like the nurses than I have trying to act like a mother.

It feels like final exams the week before school's out.

The boys have passed their hearing tests. They have passed their car-seat tests, the test that has to be performed on all preemies under a certain weight to make sure they can still breathe on the incline of the seat. It's a simple test. They feed the baby, stick him in a car seat and monitor him for ninety minutes. If the baby stops breathing before the ninety minutes is up, he fails the test. Wagner passed on his first try. Michael passed on his second. Now it's up to the twins. In order to be cleared for discharge, they need to have five consecutive days without apneas, bradys, or major de-sats.

Michael has a de-sat on the third day and the clock is restarted. And even though I know that Wagner has had five perfect days, it still takes me by surprise when a nurse comes into the boys' room and says, "If you're ready with Wagner's car seat, the doctor can finish signing the papers and he can be out of here by noon."

In my head I've queued up my joke about getting laid off as a NICU mom, but instead of wry quips I burst into tears.

"Oh, honey," she says, putting her arm around me. "Your boys are going to be okay. They're going home. Why are you crying?"

I blurt out the only answer that makes sense to me. "Because I couldn't cry before."

She nods. "That's what I did when my dad died," she says. "I couldn't cry until later. But look at them! Wagner's ready to go home."

I call Matt at work, "Wagner is coming home today!"

"*Today?*"

"Today!"

It's so sudden. I'm not even sure how to negotiate the logistics of having two children at home. How will I pick up Chiara from daycare if I have Wagner with me? Just the thought of going from the sterilized environment of the NICU to the germ-farm of Chiara's preschool makes me ill. How can I take Wagner home without Matt here to witness and celebrate? And what am I going to do with *three* kids at home? I can barely carry one infant car seat up the steep staircase that leads from our front door to the rest of our apartment on the second floor. How am I going to manage with boys in *two* infant car seats?

For a moment I'm wondering if we could just leave them here a little while longer. Like until kindergarten.

At home I pace from room to room. There will be babies here. *Here.* Sleeping here. Eating here. Living here. There's so much to do. We have to assemble the crib. We need to wash all the bottles. We have to buy diapers. And baby wipes. And bulk-sized bottles of hand-sanitizer for every room. I assemble a cart from IKEA that looks like the one the nurses have at the NICU and fill it with baby paraphernalia.

Until now we have not taken any photographs of the NICU. We

have a handful of photos the nurses have taken—Michael and Wagner shortly after they were born, Michael after his bath, nurses handing Wagner to me for the first time. All moments other people decided to memorialize.

But today we bring out the camera. We take a picture of the banner Chiara and I have made for the twins: "Welcome home, Michael and Wagner!" We take a picture of Chiara sitting in our new minivan as we drive to the hospital.

Chiara is still not permitted inside the nursery. She waits with Matt at the front. It's her first visit to the hospital since I was discharged in early January. Matt takes a picture of her looking at the birthday cards taped to the front desk.

"Today I'm gonna meet my brudders!" she tells Alison the nurse manager.

One by one the nurses disconnect the sensors. I take a picture of each one. Wagner has been breathing by himself for a couple of weeks now and all his nutrition comes from a bottle rather than an IV, but he is still connected to the oxygen-saturation cuff and he still has a sensor to monitor his heartbeat. When I pick him up, I twirl around. There are no cords to tangle or pull. He is untethered. He weighs nearly seven pounds. He's over four times his birth weight.

Back in the crib Michael is bundled, asleep. Can he sense that his buddy is gone? Michael has at least two more days in the NICU unless he stops breathing or has a heart irregularity. In that case, the five-day test will reset.

The nurses have made a little graduation cap out of the hospital-issue blue-and-pink striped newborn hats. The charge nurse carefully puts it on Wagner's head. I show him to Chiara.

"This is Wagner. Wagner, this is your big sister." Chiara pats his head and whispers, "Hi-ah, Wag-on-o."

A nurse hands us a diploma. It reads:

This is to certify that Wagner Kovac
On this most special day of March 30, 2010
Does hereby graduate from the NICU having successfully overcome,
With courage and determination, the obstacles that arose.

With courage and determination. That's how I want to remember my boys in the NICU—brave and confident, lying in their isolettes with courage and determination.

I put Wagner into his car seat and Matt arranges the diploma to create the illusion that he is proudly holding it himself. Our son is fast asleep. He looks exactly the way he did yesterday and the day before that and the day before that. A pink, puffy baby about the size of a newborn, even though he is three months old. In the transition from NICU crib to car seat he has not stirred, as if it is all the same to him.

It isn't all the same to us, of course. We are in charge of a baby now. And pretty soon we'll be in charge of two babies. There will be no fancy machines to tell us how well they are breathing or how much liquid they have passed. Wagner (and soon, Michael) is just another human in the world, heart beating, lungs breathing. Asleep. Content. Alive. Matt takes out the camera to snap another picture, but he puts it away instead. We have heard stories of parents who take their babies home only to bring them back to the NICU a few days later. We don't want to jinx this moment.

At home we sleep. At four-hour intervals, we copy the routine we've learned from the NICU. I hold the thermometer under Wagner's arm and record his temperature. I change his diaper while Matt heats a bottle of formula. Wagner doesn't choke as often as he used to, which means I can cradle him when I feed him.

Wagner is not a fussy baby and putting him to sleep is as easy as swaddling him in a blanket and putting him down in his new bed. It feels like such a luxury to have only one baby to care for. Matt and I take turns during the night. One of us sleeps while the other keeps vigil. Every four hours we switch places.

Two days later it's time for Michael to come home. There are presents. Selena, Michael's first nurse, sends him home with Hawaiian-print shirts she purchased on vacation last month. A red one for Michael, blue for Wagner. Grace gifts the twins matching track suits. Xian gives us tiny running shoes.

We have presents for them, too. Matt and I have spent the last few days writing cards to each of the twenty-seven doctors and primary nurses who have literally stood by the boys' side for the last ninety-three days. These are the ones we worked with at length. There are many others. Matt has baked a plate of cookies for the nurses' lounge. Matt's father, who will undergo chemotherapy soon, has sent thirty boxes of fudge to accompany the cards we've written.

It feels exactly like the *toi toi toi* gifts that dancers give each other on closing night. *Toi toi toi* is shorthand for spitting, which is not only good luck but wards off bad luck if you've accidentally summoned stage misfortune by singing in the dressing room, whistling backstage or—sin of sins—putting your pointe shoes on the dressing table. On opening night it's standard to give your partner a *toi toi toi* gift for luck. If the run of performances is long enough, you'll give a gift at the end, too.

We have a fan club with us: my dad, my stepmom Marian, and my sister Jackie have come in from El Paso. They have come to spend the Easter weekend with us. It's just an auspicious coincidence that Michael is coming home on Good Friday, a fitting bookend to the last time my family was here at Christmas.

We take pictures of our locker in the family room and a picture of the nurse turning off the power button on Michael's monitor.

It's a chance to repeat the ceremony of the NICU graduation and get it right this time. When we brought Wagner home on Wednesday, we shook hands and accepted his certificate, but we knew it wasn't good-bye.

But today is our last day. We must pack everything and take it with us. Matt clears out our locker—books, snacks, preemie clothes, his old flannel shirt. Marian carefully removes Chiara's artwork from the boys' room. Emma fills a bag with preemie formula, diapers, and vitamins.

As we carry our bags to the front where my father waits with Chiara, it occurs to me that this is not at all like the final performance or the last day of school. Perhaps we are going home, but the concerns for tomorrow are the same as today's. Are they breathing? Are they getting enough to eat? A new mother examines papers at the front desk as Brandon, the desk clerk, fastens a blue security bracelet on her wrist. I have no words of wisdom or consolation. Not for her. Not for me.

At home Jackie and Chiara dye Easter eggs while Marian and I feed babies. It takes forty-five minutes to feed each boy just six ounces. In three short hours we'll have to feed them again. My father reads a book on the couch. From time to time, he looks up and sighs. Finally he speaks.

"When they get older, tell them their story, but don't let their prematurity label them. It's not their identity."

I nod. I know what he means. My father has been telling me a version of this since the first time I went to San Francisco Ballet School.

"Who you are as a dancer is not who you are as a human being. Remember that," he'd say. "Ballet is not your entire identity. Maybe there are yardsticks for good and bad dancers, but there are no yardsticks for human worth."

This never made any sense. To me, what you did was who you

were. Especially if it was all you did. I was fifteen years old when I moved away from home to dance. I graduated from high school with the very minimum of requirements in order to make sure that I had more time for ballet, even though I knew it could compromise my chances for going to college later. If I was not a good dancer, then I was nothing. There was nothing left. Nothing else.

When I did quit dancing, my father worried. If my worth was tied to my dancing, what would I think of myself? But by that time it was freeing. I could do all the things I couldn't do before. I could gain five pounds without jeopardizing my job. I could drink beer. I could wear toenail polish and cut my hair short.

I know I was supposed to learn this lesson, that human worth is not tied to success, whatever that is. But instead I just changed the yardsticks. Being a ballet dancer counted for nothing. Going to school, using my brain instead of my muscles and bones, that was my identity. Doing well in school was success. And the fact that my ballet career had not been as glamorous as I'd hoped, well, that was just an embarrassment.

I can't imagine the boys as anything but preemies. And all we have done up to this point is measure them. How much do they weigh? How many ounces have they eaten? Breaths. Heartbeats. Consecutive days without an emergency. If this isn't the truth, the core of our identity, what is?

18

SUPER STARS

The boys sleep together in a bassinet and we've done our best to turn the living room into an approximation of what we left behind at the hospital. Our baby cart is a version of the ones in the NICU. It's stocked up with hand sanitizer, baby cream, sterilized water, wipes, diapers, thermometers, baby clothes, and a feeding/diaper log. We even have an oxygen-saturation sensor, in spite of the fact that we have no equipment to attach it to. Each room in the house has a bottle of Purell near the doorway the way other buildings have fire extinguishers and, when we aren't tending to babies, we walk from room to room sanitizing our hands.

Each night is divided into three shifts of four hours. The guest gets the easy shift: 8 p.m. to midnight. I take midnight to 4 a.m. Matt is on the hook from 4 a.m. to 8 a.m.

Duties consist of standing over the twins and verifying that they are still breathing.

This is easily confirmed, as the boys make loud, bleating goat noises when they sleep. We are assured that this is perfectly normal in preemies and that it, like the boys' toaster heads, will go away before they go to kindergarten.

When we aren't washing hands or counting breaths, we make bottles and feed babies. Wagner's bottles are blue; Michael's are red. They are color coded because we are sleep-deprived and new at our posts and often our only clue as to which baby was last fed is the color of the empty bottle on the counter. So far our system has worked great; only once did we feed one baby twice rather than each baby once.

We have amassed all kinds of insider knowledge. For example, we know that the preemie formula has to be mixed the day before because it gets foamy and gassy when you shake it. We know which neighborhood pharmacy carries the vitamins we have to add to their bottles and that we'll go through about twelve bottles a day. My sister has discovered that if she props a cushion against her knee and props a baby against the cushion, she can feed both twins at the same time. I have mastered the art of double-breast nursing and simultaneously reading. We think we are amazing.

Lila, the county nurse, is scheduled to visit us once a month. Her job is to make house calls to monitor babies like ours. She makes sure that we go to the doctor regularly and that we schedule appointments for the boys' RSV vaccines, especially since we have a child in preschool. Respiratory syncytial virus, or RSV for short, looks like a common cold in a healthy kid like Chiara but it can be deadly to the twins, who have compromised immune systems.

Lila weighs Wagner and marks his weight gain. We've been out of the NICU for a month now and both boys average nearly nine ounces each meal.

I can't help comparing them to Chiara when she was a month old. Every day it seemed as if she discovered something new. Her eyes focused. She reached and grasped. She turned her head to find me when she heard my voice. The boys aren't doing any of this. Lila doesn't seem worried, however.

"They're doing so we-ell! Everybody's doing soooooo we-ell!" Lila tells me.

* * * * *

My brother comes to visit with his children for Memorial Day weekend. It's exactly one year after he and his family came to visit for my graduation.

"I'll give you a tour of the NICU," I tell Jeff. It's not an invitation; it's an order. Matt stays behind with the older kids while Jeff and I take the twins to the NICU to show them off. It won't be our first visit back to the NICU. We go at least once a week and I'm not sure why. Maybe I need the reassurance of the nurses that the boys are still healthy enough to come home with me. We hover around the little lounge just inside the nursery. We look like beggars asking for attention rather than spare change.

"We were just like you!" our faces say. "But take heart. This is the place where miracles happen. Look! We are proof!"

As my brother walks slowly through the hospital halls, I try to take it in the way it must look to him—rows of sterile rooms masquerading as a baby nursery. There are framed watercolors of bunnies and pastel-colored rocking chairs alongside ventilators, portable X-ray machines, and empty isolettes. His face contorts, as if he might vomit.

"Wow," he whispers, shaking his head. "I can't even imagine what you went through."

I don't want him to picture the fear and uncertainty; I want him to picture the victory, the happy ending.

"It wasn't as bad as it looks," I say.

A voice in blue scrubs calls out from down the hall.

"Hey! The twins are here!"

We are recognized. This is my favorite part about coming back to the NICU—the doctors and nurses who crowd around. "They're so big! They're so chubby! You guys look great! You're doing so we-ell!"

Michael whimpers. Time to eat. While one of the nurses takes my brother on a tour of the back rooms, I settle into a couch in the family lounge with a red bottle.

A bedraggled father with a blue bracelet shuffles past me to the sink. He looks to be about twenty years old and his eyes never leave the floor. He has the slow resignation of a dad who's new to the NICU, and while I have no way of knowing for sure, chances are good that our boys were born earlier and smaller.

"These boys were born at twenty-five weeks and four days," I tell him. I turn Michael to face the new dad. "He weighed one pound twelve ounces and his brother weighed a pound and a half. That was four months ago. Look at them now!"

The young man's face lights up. Instead of washing his hands he runs to the bathroom door and pounds on it.

"Hurry up, Elena!" he says in Spanish to a woman inside. "I have to show you something!"

The mother emerges, still wearing her hospital gown. She is young, like the father.

I show her Michael. "We were here for three months," I say. "Babies are very resilient."

She clasps her hands to her chest and nods.

"Thank you," she says.

My brother returns from his NICU tour. He shakes his head. "I can't even imagine it," he repeats.

19

ON TOUR

We'd heard that many micro preemies aren't allowed to fly during the first two years. Too many germs. But as long as we don't go during flu season, which officially starts in October and ends in April, our pediatrician has given us permission to travel. This summer we've been to Los Angeles, El Paso, Austin, and St. Paul, Minnesota. Now we're headed to Chicago and Lake Michigan for the Kovac Family annual reunion.

Every Labor Day Matt's Aunt Rita opens her home to over fifty Kovac cousins and family friends. Just one year ago I was here at the jigsaw-puzzle table, one of four pregnant cousins, and now I am one of four new moms. I try not to compare the twins to the other babies. I try not to notice who is rolling over already and who is sitting up. Our boys were supposed to be the youngest of the new crop but instead they are the oldest by over a month. I have to remind myself that while their chronological age is eight months, their adjusted age is only four and a half months. They are still on target, even if they don't turn their heads to look at me the way the other Kovac babies crane their heads to look at their mommies. We'll get there someday, I remind myself. It's not a race.

Chiara has made herself at home.

"Can I help?" she asks Aunt Mary, who promptly gives her the task of sorting blueberries for a pie she's baking.

I have saved our cutest outfits for the reunion. For Friday they have their matching blue and red Hawaiian shirts. For Saturday they will wear their "Thing 1" and "Thing 2" outfits and on Sunday I'll dress them in the onesies from Aunt Cathy that say, "Give PEAS a Chance!"

There's a part of me that feels pushy—the way I'd act in auditions, planting myself in the front so I'd be seen. I'm trying to steal the stage from the other moms and their adorable babies. I can't help myself. I need the validation that my boys are big and strong, too.

"We were here at the house for New Year's Eve when we got the email," Aunt Rita recalls. "Howard announced, 'The twins are here!' and we said, 'the twins are here!' and then we said . . ." she lowers her voice. "Ohhhh. The twins are here. But look at them now. You'd never know they were preemies!"

I smile proudly as I hoist Wagner onto my hip. He gurgles and chews on his fist.

"You know, the nurses still talk about that edible bouquet you got for them. They'd never seen anything like it."

Rita brushes away the compliment the way you shoo away a fly. "I'm just so glad the boys are okay."

★ ★ ★ ★ ★

On Sunday morning, while the rest of the Kovacs are sunning themselves on the shores of Lake Michigan or playing cards at the house or helping Aunt Mary sort blueberries for the next pie, I am cloistered in the one corner of our beach house that gets a cell phone signal. I'm calling into a radio show along with a renowned neonatologist from our NICU. Today's program is dedicated to preemies and the stress that their parents might feel and I have been asked to give the parent perspective.

The best thing about this opportunity is that it has allowed me to slip NICU talk into casual conversation throughout the weekend without sounding like the needy mom that I am.

Things such as, "Sunday morning? Oh, I'd love to go swimming but I'm getting interviewed on this radio show. You know, to talk about the whole NICU thing."

And, "Monday morning? I'd love to but I'm appearing on a radio show to talk about being a NICU Mom. Oh, wait. The show is Sunday. Not Monday."

I am shameless.

"My guests this morning are Dr. Louise Samson, a neonatologist, and Janine Kovac, the mother of twins born three-and-a-half months early. Thank you both for making time for us today."

Dr. Samson and I, both calling in from different vacation spots, murmur our mutual thanks.

"Dr. Samson, why don't you tell us some of the risks that these tiny babies face?"

The doctor clears her throat. "Obviously the earlier the babies are born the smaller they are and the more risks they face. Typically a baby born at twenty-five weeks faces a fifty-fifty chance of survival and those that survive have a fifty percent chance of major disability. They could be blind, deaf, or have cerebral palsy, to name a few things."

She rattles off a series of acronyms and I recall the corresponding ailments. ROP refers to the arteries of the eyes that get blown out from too much oxygen. PDA—the boys had that, and then surgery to close it. NEC is short for necrotizing enterocolitis, a common and serious disease that results from dying intestinal tissue and sometimes requires surgery to stitch the healthy tissue together. Just last week a woman stopped me in the street to tell me about her twins—now twelve years old—who were born at 30 weeks. The girl was fine, but her boy had had NEC.

Dr. Samson continues. "And of course there are cognitive risks as well. Sixty-eight percent of all babies born at twenty-five weeks still have notable cognitive difficulties at age 19."

I feel my heart in my throat.

"Thank you, Dr. Samson. Wow, that's a lot. Janine, why don't you tell us what you did to help you through such a stressful time?"

"Well, uh." My mind is spinning. "A lot of what I did was try to ignore statistics like that." I try to chuckle but it comes out like a cough. "Um…I'd tell myself that each baby is an individual."

My voice gets higher and higher, as if I don't know the answer, as if I'm just guessing.

"We tried to focus on how we could be proactive in the NICU? Change diapers? Hold the babies?"

Meanwhile, my brain reels. Sixty-eight percent of babies born at twenty-five weeks still have notable cognitive disabilities 19 years later? If this were Vegas, I would have walked away from the tables rather than play. I feel wobbly and slightly nauseous. I just want to hold my boys. I don't say anything for the rest of the interview.

When I finally hang up, I'm ready to burst into tears. But I don't want to cry alone. I need to talk to Matt. I want to cry in his arms and feel him comfort me. I want us to share this together—the way we've shared everything else from reading about monoamniotic-monochorionic twins to cutting off our blue security bracelets from the NICU.

I trot down to the beach. Uncles and aunts read books from nylon beach chairs and young cousins splash in the cool deep blue of Lake Michigan. An ice chest with beer, wine, and soda sits in the shade of an umbrella. Chiara methodically pours water on a castle-in-progress from a little neon green bucket while her daddy naps on a turquoise beach towel. Our talk will have to wait until later.

My father-in-law Mike sits with Michael and Wagner in the shade under a large blue-and-yellow striped beach umbrella. He doesn't look like someone who will die from cancer a year and a half from now. To me he looks just the way I've known him these last ten years but with less hair.

The twins lie on their backs, kicking their feet, gurgling at Grandpa. Unlike the other baby cousins who are four months old and rolling around, my boys are stationary.

"How'd it go?" Mike asks.

"Harder than I thought," I reply, hoping he won't ask any follow-up questions.

"Do your little guys like the water?" He motions to the lake. His head is shiny. He finished chemotherapy in June, but his hair hasn't grown back yet.

"I know they like the pool," I answer. "But we can't be in the sun for very long. Their skin is too sensitive for sunscreen."

"Maybe just two minutes?"

"Two minutes is fine." I grin.

We each pick up a twin and walk down to the water. There's so much I don't know. I don't know exactly how many rounds of radiation Mike has had. Or how many trials of chemo. Two? Three? I prefer to think of the repeated procedures as precautionary treatments. I want to tell him that we always knew he'd make a complete recovery.

We pass a couple lounging on their faded beach towels.

"Are those twins?" the mother asks. "We have twins. Girls."

Mike the proud grandfather plays up his role. "These boys were born at twenty-five weeks." He nods at his namesake. "Can you believe it?"

The woman looks startled. "Our twins were preemies, too. They're two years old now but they were born at twenty-seven weeks."

I've never met preemies who are now toddlers. I only hear stories.

I look around for twins. What do they look like? Did they have a PDA surgery, too? Is the scar still visible? Do they need lots of sunscreen?

Reading my mind, the man says, "They're not with us. They're with my parents."

"It's our first weekend away since they were born," the woman says sheepishly.

Last week I would have asked them how their kids are doing, but the morning's radio program has reminded me how many terrible outcomes there can be.

"Well, congratulations. Well deserved, I'm sure." Mike always knows the right thing to say.

"Two years old, huh? Adjusted or chronological?"

The woman shrugs. "Adjusted, but you know, they're not walking yet or anything. And the little one has CP. Cerebral palsy." She says it like it's an apology.

The man is quick to recover. "But we had great nurses. We still go back to see them."

We compare notes. Yes, we're doing infant massage and yes, our hospital also offers the early intervention meetings that are disguised as preemie-grad playgroups. One week we meet with an occupational therapist who looks at fine motor skills. One week we meet with a speech therapist who looks at the babies' sucking reflexes. One week we meet with a physical therapist. But I can't ask the questions I really want to know: When did you know your daughter had CP? And why isn't the other one walking yet? Is that normal? Will that happen to us?

Suddenly it occurs to me that we've been in the sun a lot longer than two minutes. I nod to the baby in my arms.

"We should be getting back to the shade. Enjoy the rest of your weekend," I say, trying to sound cheerful.

"Congratulations!" the dad calls out to us as we head back to the umbrella.

20

SACRIFICE

I can't get rid of the feeling that we don't deserve to be this lucky. There is still so much that we don't know about the boys' cognitive and physical development, but we know that their organs are intact. They don't show signs of asthma or cerebral palsy. They are on target for their adjusted age. They can see. They are alive.

How are we different from that couple on the beach?

I should be relieved, but instead I feel that because our good fortune has not been earned, the boys' health could quickly take a turn for the worse. I feel like I have stolen something. I try to compensate for this irrational feeling of survivor's guilt by giving things away. So far I've donated hand-me-down clothes, books, ten bucks to a man on the corner. I even baked a batch of cookies and gave them to the workers at the Department of Motor Vehicles near our house.

I don't feel any different. If anything, my giving feels insufficient. And leaves me feeling a little embarrassed. Those people at the DMV thought I was crazy.

Maybe I'm supposed to feel embarrassed. Maybe discomfort is part of repaying the debt. Regardless, it doesn't feel like it's enough. Giving my time to volunteer for the NICU doesn't feel like enough. I need to do more, something dramatic and sacrificial, the equivalent of throwing the virgin into the volcano.

We don't have volcanoes in Oakland. For me, the most extreme offering would be to give away all my pointe shoes.

But first I have to find them. The twins are napping. I've got at least an hour to finish my search. Our second-floor apartment is tiny—we've only got four closets in the whole place, and yet I still can't find the unlabeled cardboard box that contains 21 pairs of brand new pointe shoes. Over two thousand dollars' worth of special order Freeds.

I haven't filled out a special order form in over a decade, but I still remember my specs. Vamps: 2½ inches long, "U"-cut not "V"-cut. Wing block. Sides: 1¼ inches. Heels: 1¾ inches. Shanks: 2.5mm double red-card. Extra paste in the tips.

My favorite cobbler, Maker C, had a six-month waitlist if you ordered from the United States. To get my shoes faster when I was dancing in California or Texas, I'd fax my order through my European contact.

Sometimes it took four months or longer to get your special order shoes. In the interim you'd have to wear what they call "stock shoes," which are just standard pointe shoes. Like buying off the rack. Stock shoes were clunky. The vamps were too short. The sides and heels were too high. The single red card would always bend in the wrong place. They often came from shoemakers whose craftsmanship wasn't on par with a cobbler such as Maker C, who only made special orders. The difference in quality was noticeable. You had to stay on top of your shoe order to make sure you didn't get stuck dancing in stock shoes for the first several months at a new company.

Maker C was consistent. He made shoes for wide feet, like mine. Other makers, such as P, N, and Rabbit's Teeth, made narrower shoes, even when they were given the same specs. Some makers just made shoes that fell apart right away. Like the shoemaker whose stamp was a martini glass. There were other makers I liked: M, Bell, Triangle-on-Pointe. But Maker C was my favorite.

Some dancers would go through a pair of pointe shoes in a single rehearsal, but I was always miserly with my shoes. I could make them last a whole week, sometimes even three. I'd wear as many as six different pairs in a day, alternating shoes after an hour of rehearsal to make them last longer, stretching their three-week duration over the course of three months.

I wonder how my shoe specs would have been different if I'd had a more secure ballet career. I would love to have been one of those dancers who didn't give her shoes a second thought. Who didn't try to squeeze thirty more minutes out of each pair by staggering their use during the week. I'd have ordered single red cards instead of double. I would have foregone the extra paste in the tips and the wing block. Some of my friends would take a pair, hastily stitch elastics and ribbons, bang the shoes on the sidewalk before class and then discard them at the end of the day.

I never did that. Each pair of Freeds—each shoe—was examined and caressed. Sewing them was a ritual. First I'd cut the satin off the tips with my single-edged razor blade. Then I'd darn them with dental floss. I'd pick out thread—something colorful to help me differentiate between pairs. Green, pink, blue, red. I'd pore over picking out the right elastic (not too thick, not too stretchy). The right ribbons, hopefully with one shiny side and one dull side to minimize slippage. When a pair of shoes was "dead," I'd carefully cut off the elastics and ribbons to reuse them for the next pair.

Sifting through the closets is a journey back in time. There is a box of term papers from my freshman year when I'd tried to stand out by using an unorthodox font and olive-green ink. I didn't even know that I needed to double-space my papers. The last time I'd handed in a paper before going to college, I'd typed it on an IBM Selectric typewriter.

There is a box of cassette tapes from Matt's previous life as a heavy metal fan. A box of memorabilia from both of our careers. Yellowed newspaper clippings. Some in English, others in Italian, Icelandic, and even in Chinese. There is a box of receipts and cards including one from the ballet master during my days in Reykjavik that reads, "Yes, everybody loves you. Stop being such a social butterfly and get back in the studio."

And then—finally, The Box. I can tell. Brown. Nondescript. Squashed on one side. Two feet by two feet. It looks exactly the same as it did when it sat in a corner of my old studio apartment.

I couldn't bear to look at it then. Some pairs had already been labeled with smiley faces and exclamation points and shellacked with acrylic cement before getting boxed away. Other shoes arrived after I'd started the computer programming certification process that would give me a second career. I knew by then I'd never be a professional ballet dancer again. At thirty, I was too old to go through rehab and then get back into competitive shape. There was no company waiting for me to get better. No mentor encouraging me to come back. I'd shoved the box in the corner. Just the thought of all those years, saving up my pointe shoes only to have a surplus I'd never use, made the hair on the back of my neck prickle like that of an angry cat.

But over the years my attitude had softened, and rather than being a symbol of what I never accomplished, the shoes became a symbol of what I might still do. I could get in shape again. Someday. Not to dance professionally. Just to dance. I could start with occasional ballet classes at the studio next door. Maybe work my way back to a Saturday class at one of the professional studios in San Francisco. A part of me still wants to wait for someday. Another part feels like this is the perfect atonement. Sometimes giving should hurt.

I want to find the perfect recipient for my shoes. Someone who really needs them, who can appreciate them, who would never be able to afford them otherwise, someone desperate for pointe shoes. The way I was once. I try to picture the dancer's face. What will she think of her good luck? Will she wonder about me? *Who was this dancer who had such perfect shoes?* I want my gift to be anonymous. My last name is printed in block letters on the leather soles of the shoes, but I go by my married name now. YouTube and Google didn't exist when I was dancing. There's no Internet proof that I was ever a dancer. No way to trace the shoes to me. I like this cloak of anonymity. It makes the gift that much more selfless.

I put the box on the floor. I feel warm and fuzzy and sentimental and proud. My life is in there. Each corner of the box is folded under another flap so that opening it is like a flower blossoming. There they are: twenty-one pairs of special order Freeds. Some pairs are white satin, which are even more glorious than the signature peach-pink of the regular Freeds.

The first thing I notice is the luxurious smell of leather and cobbler's glue. The shoes smell the same as they did when I was thirteen, sewing my first pair on my skinny little bed. It's the same smell I came home to every day, whether it was El Paso, Seattle, Reykjavik, Verona, or San Francisco; my shoes were always lined up on their tips along the baseboard in the bedroom. It's the smell that says, "With enough care and diligence, you can do anything."

The next thing I notice is the dust. Not the gray dust of a neglected house but tiny brown crumbs that look like cinnamon that doesn't smudge. It doesn't look like the glue that sometimes coagulates on the inside of the shoes where the canvas meets the shanks and it doesn't look like dirt.

Then I notice little black dots. Tons of them, lining the satin on the outside of my shoes and dotted along the canvas on the inside. They are scarcely bigger than a speck. Some are perfectly symmetrical and others are not. The symmetrical specks do not brush away.

The non-symmetrical ones are moving.

Bugs.

Bugs in my *shoes*.

They are everywhere. Crawling. Eating. Laying eggs. Leaving brown dust. Desecrating my perfectly made Maker C shoes. The whole time I thought I was preserving the pristine artifacts from my career, my shoes were being eaten away by bugs.

I turn the box upside down and forty-two shoes tumble out. The bugs have probably been eating away at my shoes for years, but in my mind it's as if they've just started. As though the shoes have suddenly ignited and if I act quickly enough, I can put out the fire. I jump to attention; I want to save what's left. But I'm also disgusted. The brown "dust" is probably bug excrement, I realize. I shake each shoe vigorously upside-down, dumping out bugs and bug shit. Some bugs I flick away. Others I squash with my thumbnail.

If it were anything else—books or clothes or photographs—I would have thrown them in the garbage rather than clean away bugs. But these are my precious pointe shoes. With a wet paper towel I brush the satin of each shoe, caressing and assessing the damage. The canvas on the inside is brittle. There are tiny holes where the satin has been eaten away. Are they still usable? How long have bugs been eating away at them?

I'd been excited to give away my shoes, but now I just want to get rid of them. My selfless offering is not beauty but trash. Who would want these now? I put them back into the plain brown, slightly squished box and carry it down the stairs. I leave it on the sidewalk outside the door with a sign: FREE SHOES.

My mind is still on the shoes when the twins and I go for our afternoon walk. They are too little for the fancy double stroller the women at work gifted to Matt. We're still using the bucket seats that snap into a double stroller frame. It means that to get us out the door, I have to make three trips down the stairs. First I take down the stroller frame and park it next to my box of bug-eaten shoes, double-checking the brake. Next, I carry Michael in his infant car seat. Matt can take both car seats at the same time, but I'm not strong enough. I have no choice but to snap Michael into the stroller frame and leave him alone on the sidewalk while I carry Wagner down in his car seat. The boys are getting heavier and I'm always afraid I'm going to tumble down our long flight of stairs head-over-heels, baby, car seat and all.

I release the brake and push the stroller to the corner, leaving the box by our doorstep. When I approach the ballet studio next door, I peer through the frosted glass. The lights are off; it's too early for classes to start. But later this afternoon, the piano music from *pliés* and *tendus* will float up through my kitchen window. I'll hear it while washing bottles and cutting carrots for Chiara's snack.

I could do it. I could get back in shape. I could even wear those shoes again. I'd start the way I did when I was eleven. Five minutes a day, adding five more minutes each week. Building up strength. Getting those calluses back. I'm not too old.

I'm not even halfway around the block when I decide to turn back. My shoes aren't just a symbol of what I accomplished in my career; they're a symbol of what I can still do. Besides, no one else could love those shoes the way I did. This was a sign that it's never too late. I don't need sacrifice to feel better. I just need to seize the day. I could start on Monday. I could be back in the studio doing triple pirouettes by Christmas. When the studio opens, I'll sign up for classes again. Chiara, too.

When I get to my front door, the box is gone. I don't know if I'm relieved or disappointed. I carry the car seats back up the stairs, first Wagner, then Michael, cautiously, one step at a time. The carpool drops Chiara off from her preschool. I cut carrots in the kitchen and look out over the courtyard of the ballet studio below. When the piano music drifts into the apartment, I close the window to shut it out.

21

BRACING FOR IMPACT

By Halloween we have reached a new level of normal. The summer guests who helped us through twin 4 a.m. feedings are long gone and the guest room is now the boys' room. Matt has duct-taped together parts from two IKEA cribs to create one big crib. It looks more like a padded toddler wrestling ring than a crib, but it's big enough for an adult to climb into and read books and cuddle. I'm sure some day we'll give them their own beds but I can't help but try to compensate for the cohabitation time that they missed.

We have discovered that when one cries in the night he only wakes up his brother when Matt or I come to soothe the crier. As if it is more disruptive to know your twin is getting comforted and fed than it is to listen to him yell. Which means that we either have to let our boys cry it out or both of us have to answer the call. Two babies, two parents, two bottles. On any given night there's a fifty-fifty chance that one of us wakes up in the crib. At least it's nice to know we can co-sleep and be reassured that no one will fall out of bed.

Chiara spends nearly as much time as we do in the boys' crib. Last week, just before their late afternoon nap, the twins were fussy, making noncommittal cries. Chiara climbed into the crib and sat between them. She put a hand on the chest of each baby. She looked so much older than her three-and-a-half years.

"It's okay. You're okay," she said in a soothing voice. "I'm right here."

When they are awake, she educates them. She shows them her princess collection. "This is Sleeping Beauty. And this one is Cinderella."

She shows them photographs. "This is me with my mommy and daddy."

She reassures them. "Don't worry. You aren't going to die for a really long time."

She helps with baths. She picks out their clothes. She brings me wipes and diapers when it's time to change them. "It looks like a chicken!" she giggles, referring to the body parts that she doesn't have.

When one of them cries, she comes running to me, always assuming that they need to be fed. "Mama! Mama! They're starving! My brudders are starving!"

She reads them books and makes up stories. "This is the story of when Pooh Bear died. One day Christopher Robin found him drowned in a pool of water."

From time to time she holds tea parties, elaborate picnics of wooden food and imaginary lemonade. Babies are not allowed to come to these soirées. Only mommies and daddies. But for the most part she has embraced her role as big sister.

Meanwhile, her room has become a hospital ward for sick dolls. Some of them have colds. Some of them have cancer. She is the doctor and because I am the one who can read and write, I am the charge nurse. When she plays hospital, I have to shadow her and take notes. She is amazingly organized for a three-year-old. Each doll has a manila folder with its name and ailment and various medications Dr. Strawberry has prescribed. When she is done playing for the day she stacks all the folders on top of her doctor's kit.

Perhaps she remembers the nurses and doctors from my time in the hospital. Perhaps she has simply extended her knowledge from her own experience with the pediatrician. A dozen dolls lie in shoeboxes and makeshift beds scattered around her room. Baby Elizabeth has had a headache for three weeks now. Baby Juna has a sore throat. Baby Lala died.

I dutifully write the dolls' names on the folders, but I cheat when it comes to recording illnesses. I can't bear to write "tummy cancer" on Baby Nellie's file. I write scribbles and doodles instead. After all, it's not like Chiara can tell the difference. She doesn't even know the letters of the alphabet. And hopefully by the time she does learn the difference, she'll be out of this phase.

I don't know if this is typical three-year-old behavior, if this is to be expected after everything we have been through this year. But each sick doll, each macabre story of mortality, is handled matter-of-factly. I think I'd be more worried if there were panic or regret or any emotion at all. So I tell myself this just must be how three-year-olds process life events around them. Besides, she did the exact same thing last year during potty training when her Snow White doll peed in the pool, much to the chagrin of the Little Mermaid.

"Next time tell me when you need to go," she'd scolded as she took Snow White out of the shoebox pool.

While I don't know about typically developing three-year-olds, I do know about typically developing babies. I hold two ages in my head. Chronologically the boys are eleven months old. But for their adjusted age, they really are eight months old. Staying true to the active baby he was in the womb, Michael starts crawling six weeks before his brother. He crawls in circles around Wagner, who has discovered that as the center of Michael's orbit, the toys come to him.

Wagner, on the other hand, is first to master rolling. He lies on his back, arches, and then slowly rolls to his side where he stays for just a split second before continuing to roll onto his tummy. When he successfully rolls without banging his chin, he laughs maniacally and quickly rolls to his back to practice again. He's rehearsing, I think to myself.

However, neither one of them responds to language. "Hi." "Bye." "Mama." "Cookie." Nothing provokes a reaction. Chiara didn't start talking until she was a year old, but she knew the word "cookie" before she could crawl over to get one. I know all babies progress at different rates, but it's hard to be patient. And just last month, at the boys' first NICU follow-up appointment, we discovered that neither one responds to noises from sources they cannot see. In other words, if you stand behind them and clap your hands, they do not turn toward the sound. It's perfectly normal, we are assured. Our babies spent the first three months of life shutting out the noises around them. They'll catch up, the doctor tells us.

Matt still sleeps with his cell phone in his pajamas in case the NICU calls in the middle of the night, even though there is no reason to call us. It will be another month before he will sleep without it.

Every morning he wakes up early with the boys and reads to them. "Dog." "Cat." "Bike."

"The wheels on the bus go round and round," he sings over and over. "See the bus? That's a bus. Buuuuus."

The boys' lack of language is more worrisome to him than it is to me. He's hoping his daily morning story hour will make a difference. The boys sit contentedly chewing on whatever volume is not being read at the moment. They'll listen to Matt read *The Wheels on the Bus* for thirty minutes and while we should find their long attention span comforting, we don't. This behavior is so atypical that Matt's convinced it's an indication of another problem, one we don't see yet, one that will manifest itself later. Maybe they are on the autism spectrum. Or perhaps they just have a hard time processing the sounds they hear.

We need to train ourselves to be happy with worst-case scenarios. Just in case. If I had any sense of self-reflection I might notice that I have no emotional reflexes left but my physical reflexes are amazing. I can rescue a toppling wine goblet two seats away without spilling a drop. And when a treasured black ceramic bowl shatters on to the floor, spilling peas everywhere, I don't jump or curse. I barely blink.

"Guess we'll have corn tonight!" I say as I float over to the broom and sweep up black shards and green peas.

But life isn't all walking on eggshells. We have an arsenal of jokes at the ready.

When people ask, "How do you tell them apart?" we answer, "Well, we only circumcised one of them."

Sometimes Matt varies it with a political response: "Michael's very conservative; Wagner's a libertarian." I think it would be funnier to say that Wagner's a socialist. But Matt disagrees.

Or, when one of them falls at the playground: "It's okay. We have a spare." This gem gets recycled whenever guests express concern that we haven't baby-proofed the stairs.

Other times we drudge up this nugget from our NICU days: "They'll be growing more lung tissue over the next ten years so we figure this is the best time for them to smoke."

We get fewer and fewer laughs, but whether it's because folks have heard our jokes already or because they were never funny in the first place, it's hard to say. You'd think that if audience reaction didn't deter us, at least it would motivate us to make up some new jokes, but it doesn't. Maybe it's not funny to us, either. Maybe we're still on auto-pilot. But at least when we're trying to be funny, we're not focused on all that's really worrying us.

* * * * *

It's the day after Thanksgiving. Michael's asleep. Matt has *Nutcracker* performances in Mountain View, an hour south of Oakland.

Chiara and I will see him dance tomorrow. We'll bring the boys with us. There are always mothers backstage eager to hold babies, especially chubby ones who sit still for thirty minutes chewing on books.

"I'm going to make dinner," I tell Chiara. "Don't let Wagner crawl away." It's a joke that would be funnier if there were another adult around, but Chiara is too little to understand that Wagner is basically stationary. Sometimes I have to be my own audience.

Chiara nods and crouches to Wagner's level. "Would you like to hear a story?" she asks him, to no reaction.

I'm in the kitchen making baby food. I should wake Michael up from his nap but then I'd never get dinner finished. Even though I'm just reheating leftovers, Michael is hard to keep an eye on. He's always in motion. Just as I'm wondering if this relative quiet is good news or bad news, I hear a loud bumping noise, as if all of our shoes have cascaded down the stairs to our front door. I freeze. What if it's not shoes?

Chiara yells, "Mama! Mama!" I'm getting ready to laugh and reassure her when she runs into the kitchen. "Oh, my goodness! Oh my goodness! Wagner is falling down the stairs!"

By the time we get to the staircase, Wagner is at the bottom. I run so fast I feel like I'm flying. For a split second I picture both of us at the bottom of the stairs, our skulls cracked open, blood everywhere. Chiara, looking down at us. What would she do? She doesn't even know how to call 911.

Wagner is wide-eyed and screaming. He looks surprised. No blood. No cracked skull.

I scoop him up and take him to the bedroom.

I am so stupid. What the hell was I thinking? Did I really expect Chiara to watch him?

I hold Wagner until he stops crying. It's a familiar place for us—me comforting my son through deep breaths and warm hands. Shit. We get through three months in intensive care, and then I do a dumbshit thing and he ends up brain damaged anyway.

"Chiara, honey, can you get me the phone?"

She stands in the doorway. She looks so tiny. Two years from now she will tell her brother her version of the fall as she remembers it. "One day you fell down the stairs. And I flew down the stairs like an angel and caught you in my arms and saved you."

"Which phone? The one in the living room or the one in the kitchen?"

It takes me a moment to understand her question. Of course, our landline has two phones in two cradles at opposite sides of the apartment. Why would Chiara assume that they are the same? She's only three years old. Shit. How could I have left her to watch Wagner?

"The living room phone. Thank you, sweetie. Want to see if Michael is awake? Want to read him some books?" I don't want her to hear my phone call with the nurse.

She is full of reassurances. Wagner has a bruise on his forehead, but that's it. No bleeding, no dents, no bruises on his body. He is asleep.

"Kids fall all the time. He's probably fine. But come in on Monday and we'll check him out anyway. And be sure to go to the emergency room if it looks like he has a concussion."

That's the conversation I recount to Matt when I call him on the phone. I save the first question I got from the advice nurse for later that night when I can tell him face-to-face.

"Does he recognize you?" the nurse had said.

"How would I know that?" I'd responded.

"Does he know you're his mother?" she rephrased.

That's when my heart dropped. Not because the answer was *no* but because I realized that my son is eleven months old and the answer has always been *no*.

The nurse tried again. "Does he seem comforted by you or is he scared of you?"

Yes, he is comforted by me. Wagner and I have always been able to comfort each other. From his first days as a micro preemie with his breathing tubes and heart monitor, his IV and phototherapy lights, he was always comforted by the sound of my voice. We knew because the oxygen-saturation numbers on the monitor told us so. They told us that Wagner breathed more deeply when he heard my voice or felt my touch.

But he doesn't know I am his mother.

When Matt comes home, I confess.

"I should have put a gate up weeks ago," he sighs, claiming responsibility.

"I should have been watching him," I counter.

Meanwhile, Wagner looks fine. He eats. He sleeps. He wakes up. His pupils are not dilated. He has one bruise on his forehead, which is barely visible when the pediatrician examines him two days later. He has no broken bones. No concussion. His scary fall reminds me of my own. What has happened that we can't see or won't know until later?

"Babies fall from all heights and surfaces," the doctor says. "Most of the time they're fine. But you will get that baby gate, right?"

I nod. "We already have!"

I want to ask why Wagner doesn't turn his head when Matt says, "Where's Mama?" Or why he doesn't wave "bye-bye." I know he's just eight months adjusted, but Chiara was already waving when she was eight months old. She knew words such as "banana" and "cracker," even though she couldn't say them.

In the end I lose my nerve. I'm afraid of the answer. Or worse, that there is no answer. That we'll just have to wait and see. For the next several months we will scan Wagner's eyes and watch his reaction to others. Does he recognize me yet? Does he know who we are? Does Michael? If they don't talk and don't understand words, how will we know?

22

SPINNING THE STORY

Now that flu season is here, the boys get a Synagis shot to help protect them against RSV. We see the same nurse every month and every month she exaggerates the boys' prematurity.

"Look how robust they are!" she brags to her assistant when we come in November. "Born at twenty-four weeks. Barely a pound!"

In the beginning I considered correcting her, but I felt so silly saying, "Michael wasn't born at a pound and a half. It was one pound and twelve ounces."

At Christmas she boasts that they were twenty-two-weekers and by the time flu season is over in April, the way she tells the story, my boys are twenty-weeker micro preemies born weighing half a pound.

It's such a ridiculous bending of facts. I'm not sure if this fabrication is intentional. Is it supposed to make us feel better? Or does she exaggerate because she can't remember from month to month, and to someone who works with toddlers and children, the difference between twenty weeks and twenty-five weeks and four days is negligible?

The nurse's loose relationship with the truth has given me license to exaggerate as well. Never about the facts. I never truncate "twenty-five weeks and four days" to just twenty-five weeks. But I am selective about the details that I share.

When we go to the dentist because the boys' teeth have patches where there is no enamel, I tell the hygienist that the NICU helped me catch up on my sleep.

"I didn't have to wake up and feed twins every two hours," I point out. "It was such a relief."

At the library when another mom credits her mom-and-baby yoga class with helping her build friendships with other moms, I nod.

"That's exactly how I feel about our NICU playgroup." Of course, the NICU playgroup isn't a playgroup at all. Every Tuesday parents sit with their babies and hope for positive feedback from the rotating staff of early intervention specialists. Is this the week the occupational therapist will notice a strong pincher grip or will she prescribe another set of exercises?

But the way I tell the story, it's a group of moms who get together and bond over our shared experiences. It's true enough. I've started to write down our story for posterity. I record what I remember but I also superimpose what I know now. We were never scared, I claim. I emphasize the friendships we have made with the nurses, doctors, social workers, security guards, and parking attendants. I squeeze every silver lining out of our three-month NICU stay. It's part massaging the truth, but it's also like choreographing a dance.

I don't write about the hours we logged watching the boys' monitors. Or stroking their ribcages to get them breathing again.

I don't write about the time I walked into the boys' room not knowing that their big bulky breathing machines had been replaced by small ones. "Oh. The boys died," had been my first thought, followed by, "Someone would have called me if my babies died." I let those thoughts flutter back and forth but I never give them breath.

Instead I write about Grace, the nurse whose daughter got married at Disneyland, complete with Cinderella coach. I describe Xian, who invited us to her son's birthday party, and Liam, who was a scratch golfer. Kalpana, who spent her vacations on Red Cross missions to Haiti to dispense medical aid. Dionne, who'd been a nanny for triplets. It was all about the nurses, I insist, as if our NICU tenure was a three-month cocktail party. The way I spin the story, you'd think we spent that time in a hotel, not a hospital.

When I worked with choreographers, I loved how I could match the music to steps. I loved the process of rehearsal, how rough edges were smoothed into something flawless and perfect through constant revision and repetition. You sand and polish until all that's left is the story you want to hear.

And maybe from the wings you could feel the heat from the stage lights and see the scuffs marking up the floor and the gaffer's tape between panels of Marley flooring, but from beyond the orchestra pit you don't see any of that. You can't see the dancers sweat or the marks on the soles of their pointe shoes. All the imperfections are washed out.

I never realized that I could do this with words, too. Each time I revise a sentence or tweak a phrase I soften the edges until the NICU is just a shadow.

23

ENCORE

It feels like a normal July 4th weekend. We'd hoped to introduce the boys to hot dogs and corn on the cob and maybe even take the kids to the marina and see the fireworks. But last night Wagner had a little fever. First it lingered around 100 degrees. By morning it had spiked to about 102. It isn't his first illness. Both boys have had earaches and fevers. Nothing a little infant Tylenol couldn't handle. At lunch Wagner is listless and still hot.

During nap time, I lie down with him in the big double crib. He is red. His breathing is uneven. His fever is 103.7. If the Tylenol doesn't do anything, we'll call the doctor, I tell Matt. I stroke Wagner's forehead with a wet cloth. He leans against me and closes his eyes.

By two o'clock the fever has spiked to 105.

The advice nurse from the hotline tells us, "If you don't hear from the doctor in the next two minutes, call an ambulance."

We watch the clock. After a hundred and twenty-five seconds, Matt calls 911.

Three minutes later the doctor calls.

"I don't think you needed to call an ambulance. That's a little excessive," he scolds. "Don't you live just a mile from Children's Hospital? You could have just driven to the emergency room."

"But he's a preemie," I say, giving him Wagner's birth date and adjusted age, in case he's forgotten.

"He's not a preemie anymore," the doctor counters. "He's a year and a half."

He's not a preemie anymore? The fact just hangs there in the air. *Huh.*

"But he still doesn't really talk!" As I say the words, it dawns on me that developmental delays are not the domain of emergency rooms. The doctor thinks I have overreacted. I am proud of this fact. It may be the first time I have ever overreacted.

The ambulance parks out in front. Neighbors creep onto their porches to watch.

"This is so we can get to the hospital faster," I tell Chiara. She follows us down the stairs. "So we can get help for your brother." Matt nods, mouth in a tight line.

I've never seen the inside of an ambulance before. It's bigger than I thought and I'm surprised at how many machines and gadgets I recognize. A paramedic in a steel-gray jacket takes Wagner's vital signs. 104, he records. The other paramedic just stands there, like an understudy. Wagner reaches for me. See? He does know I'm his Mama.

"It was a 105 degrees before I called," I say. I want them to know that we had a good reason for calling 911.

The paramedic in the gray jacket nods. "Then it's moving in the right direction. We'll be on our way here in just a moment, Mrs. Kovac."

He is calm and friendly, flirty, almost. He makes eye contact and uses complete sentences. When did his fever start? Has this happened before? This is my first clue that Wagner is not going to die in the next ten minutes. When the situation is dire, medical professionals get to work first and gather medical history later.

I sit in the back with the paramedic. Wagner clings to me. The understudy drives, sirens wailing.

We've never been to the ER before. Whenever we go to Children's Hospital for our monthly vaccines, we enter through the front where the murals of the giraffes and elephants are.

The admittance nurse is young and blonde. It's a slow day here at the ER. The waiting room is completely empty. She puts down her nail file and smiles. Either she knows the paramedic or he really is a flirt. He gives her Wagner's vitals, but he looks like he's reciting poetry. I almost feel like an interloper.

"Let's see what we have here. Hi, sweetie," she coos. It takes me a moment to realize she is talking to Wagner, not the paramedic.

Wagner's temperature is even lower now: 103.

"Have a seat over there." She gestures to the empty waiting room. "We'll be with you in a moment."

Now I know for sure that everything is going to be okay. If this were life or death, nobody would talk to me at all. A throng of doctors in gray scrubs and masks would materialize and whisk my baby away with them, leaving me alone outside on the pavement. This is so different from our experience of hospitals. Maybe the doctor was right. Maybe we aren't preemies anymore.

It helps that Wagner likes to snuggle when he's not feeling well. He doesn't cry or moan. He's like a kitten that just wants to be held, or a koala, clinging to me. The next day my forearm will be sore from supporting him.

Ninety minutes later we are called.

"Wagner Kovac?"

I carry Wagner to the reception desk. "Over there," the receptionist nods to an office opposite the doors that lead from the ER to the exam rooms. We're going in the wrong direction, I think.

The windowless office is dimly lit. If I didn't know better, I'd think we were in the basement.

"Insurance card and driver's license?" the receptionist asks in a monotone voice. She photocopies Wagner's insurance card and examines it against my driver's license. I'm just some mom with a chubby toddler. If there had been a problem, an inkling of a problem, no one would care about insurance at this point.

The bored receptionist gestures back to the waiting room. "They'll call you in a minute."

Everything is painstakingly slow. As if we don't matter. I am not used to not mattering when it comes to Wagner and Michael. I am used to giant fusses.

It's five o'clock. We have been here for nearly three hours. Back at home Matt is cooking dinner, wiping up milk spills, picking peas off the floor, asking Chiara for the fifth time to wash her hands, pleading with Michael to eat some food. After dinner he'll read *The Wheels on the Bus* for the 18 millionth time today and play doctor with Chiara as she makes her rounds in her bedroom. Baby Abigail has another cold. Baby Jackson still has cancer.

Meanwhile, Wagner and I sit and wait. We are very still. Like the space between deep breaths. I have nothing left to imagine. My reflexes are like fried wires. Wagner rests his head on me, looking pale and vacant and feeling like a hot potato. I have never been so still. The only power we have ever been able to harness is me holding him, his head resting on my breast. This is all we have ever been able to do. This is our secret talent, our superpower. I'm finally doing something perfectly.

"Wagner Kovac? Follow me."

We are led down the hall to a nondescript room. It's colder here.

"Hi, Wagner. I'm Brian," the nurse says to Wagner, who barely lifts his head.

The nurse puts a thermometer under Wagner's arm. He doesn't resist. Does a part of him remember that I did this several times a day, every day for the first three months after he was born? A part of my heart breaks that my little toddler is such a willing patient. The thermometer chirps. 102. It hardly even seems like a fever.

"Has he been drinking liquids?" Brian asks. I shake my head.

Brian turns to Wagner. "Would you like some water, honey?" Wagner shakes his head.

"So it looks like the fever is coming down on its own. I think we should take some blood for tests and maybe give your son an IV to hydrate him a bit."

Two years ago the thought of an IV in my child's arm would have terrified me. This time I'm thinking, "Oh, yes. Please."

Either because he's too tired or because he's too experienced, Wagner doesn't cry when one needle pulls out blood and another fills him with liquid. He only grimaces. Brian tapes a little splint to Wagner's arm. "So he doesn't pull the tubes out," he tells me.

I think of telling him that he won't because he's the Blue Baby. That Michael, the Red Baby, was the one who tugged on tubes, but I don't say anything. Suddenly I feel very empty.

"I'm going to take this down to the lab and we'll get those results back as soon as possible," Brian tells me. "If you need anything, just let me know."

Wagner lies in my arms like a sedated puppy.

It's cold. We left so quickly that I didn't think to bring a bag. Wagner isn't even wearing any pants, just a diaper. I wait for Brian to come check on us but he passes by without so much as a nod in our direction. It dawns on me. What do I think this is? A restaurant? But I know his name. I can ask him for a blanket. I bet there's a closet in this very hall with a stack of freshly laundered blankets. If it's like the NICU, those blankets are even warmed.

"Brian?" I call out.

Brian materializes in the doorway.

"Could we have a blanket?"

He returns seven seconds later with a thick, warm blanket.

"And, uh, I don't get cell reception here. Is there a phone where I could call home and tell them we're all right?"

Brian returns with a phone.

"Hey, honey," I tell Matt when he answers. "Just wanted to let you know that we're okay. Everything's okay. There's just no cell service."

"Oh, whew," he says. "That's what I was hoping. Nothing to worry about here. I just fed Michael and Chiara dinner. We'll be getting ready for bed soon." It's seven-thirty. Later he will tell me what he was really thinking during dinner: *This is what our lives would look like if one of them didn't make it.*

Instead he says, "Do you want us to pick you up when you're done?"

"Nah. We'll walk. It's not that far." I force a chuckle. "We probably didn't need that ambulance after all."

"Maybe," he agrees. "But better safe than sorry. Be careful on the walk home. We'll see you later."

Meanwhile, the IV does the job. Wagner perks up. His face is pink now and his skin isn't clammy anymore. Suddenly I'm starving. I wonder if he's hungry, too. They must have some food here.

"Hey, sweetie. Do you want to eat something?"

Wagner nods.

"I wanna cracker," he says. A perfect sentence. Subject, verb, object.

A female nurse paces through the hall. Her body language has a special alertness that makes me think that she is filling in while someone else is on his break. She consults someone, a doctor maybe, and I can tell from their whispers that someone else, a child, is in a more precarious position than we are. The nurses use one tone of voice to put the parents at ease and a different one amongst themselves.

Just as I am debating whether to interrupt them, a doctor enters.

"Hello, Wagner! I'm Dr. Folsom."

She extends her hand to me.

"I understand you had a pretty high fever," she says, as if Wagner can understand.

Then, to me: "Well, his tests look great. There's nothing here. Call us if anything changes, but as far as I'm concerned you guys are good to go. I'll get Brian to take out the IV and send you on your way. Do you have any questions?"

I should have questions. Important ones such as: Will this happen again? Can he still be sick even though the fever's gone? And the most pressing question: "How come you can't tell me what happened?"

But instead I say, "Do you have any crackers or anything? We're really hungry."

She grins. "We can do that."

All my life I've tried so hard to be something. Be good. Be calm. Be skinny. Be smart. Be on time. Right now I'm not trying to be anything. I'm just sitting in a lumpy sort of way with my son who seems kind of thick and doughy. He doesn't make any noise; he just rests his chin on my shoulder and we sit here. Maybe this will make up for all the hours I couldn't hold him. Maybe each baby needs to be held a certain number of hours and this will get us closer to filling our quota.

Maybe there is a part of Wagner that remembers a hospital as a place where his mama can just hold him.

This is how I want to remember the NICU, as lasting only five hours, not three months. As a place where our greatest needs are blankets and crackers. I want to record over the NICU memory with this one of the ER, the way you trick your brain into forgetting the steps the choreographer has discarded and retrain your muscles to remember the new version as if it's the only one that has ever existed.

At eight o'clock we begin our walk home. The night air is crisp but warm. I may have forgotten the diaper bag, but I remembered the baby carrier. I fasten Wagner into the Ergo and clock another hour of holding my baby heart-to-heart.

24

FACING THE
AUDIENCE

The pediatrician thinks that the boys' immune systems are now strong enough to withstand the carnival of germs at Chiara's daycare. This is good news because I've been accepted to a weeklong writing workshop in Tahoe. When Wagner got sick, I wasn't sure if I'd still be able to go. But a month has passed and his fever never returned.

I have expanded our story of micro preemie twins into an essay that will help parents cope when they have a baby in the NICU. Today my group will give me feedback on the piece I wrote.

The workshop is broken into groups of a dozen writers and each day we meet with an author or editor or agent who leads a discussion on the craft of writing. In our morning meetings we workshop two manuscripts from writers in the group. The afternoons are filled with panel discussions and at night there are readings and parties. At the end of the week there is a variety show, "The Follies." Students and faculty sing songs and act out skits. I'm actually considering dancing. I can't resist the opportunity to perform in front of an audience.

Back home Matt is enjoying a break between work and his first semester of law school. The twins, eighteen months in chronological age, are still only fifteen months developmentally. On their first day of day-care they fall asleep at naptime holding hands, reaching across their cots.

I've acclimated quite quickly to life without family—staying up late, drinking wine with new friends, discussing narrative structure into the wee hours. By the time my manuscript gets workshopped at the end of the week, I've found a whole new community of friends. I'm ready for feedback. After all, it'll only make my work stronger.

"Don't be nervous," my housemates tell me. Along with "Good luck! Don't listen to anything that doesn't resonate with you." And, "Remember only you can tell your story." Advice on how to take advice.

I'm not nervous. As far as I'm concerned, nothing can compare to getting corrected by dancers, especially ones who may be vying for your role, or by a director who wants your boyfriend. I know how to separate helpful, objective feedback from viciousness. And by Friday I know the writers in my group. They're a good bunch.

A well-known novelist, an agent-turned-author, sits very straight at the head of the table. She is framed by the towering peak that is the hallmark of this Squaw Valley ski resort. The mountain looks exposed without snow and skiers. The ski lift looks like a painting in which the artist went on break and didn't come back to color in the snow. The grass is dusty green and smooth black rocks peek out here and there. My group shifts in the mismatched plastic chairs, some hunter green, others beige. Our makeshift classroom sits outside in the shadow of the ski lodge. Behind us a vast parking lot looms. The blacktop soaks up the sunshine. I've brought bagels and cream cheese and I arrange them as if I'm the hostess of a party.

"Go easy on me!" I joke to my friend Dorothy and hand her an onion bagel. "Remember that I'm the one who brought you breakfast!"

I pretend to be nervous but I can't imagine that a critique of my writing could ever be as damaging as feedback on my dancing. First of all, my writing is not me. It's *out there*—on a piece of paper or on my hard drive. It's much harder to separate the dancer from the dance. Moreover, dance feedback relies on the critic's memory; it focuses on a movement in the past, a trick or illusion. Sometimes we can't even agree that we are talking about the same step, like evaluating a sand sculpture that has been washed away by the tide. But here—with writing—we can all point to the same paragraph. Even if our red pens circle different words and we have different perspectives, at least we can agree on the starting place.

"I know you all know how this works," the novelist tells the twelve writers. She doesn't even have to tell us to quiet down—she just gives the table a strong glance and lifts her chin and we all shut up like obedient second-graders. She lowers her gaze and looks at me. Her face doesn't soften but her voice does.

"Before we start I just want to tell you that my youngest was in the NICU. Not as long as your little guys. But—" she shudders and shakes her head, "it's the kind of thing you never forget."

I have a shrug and a nod prepared but her eyes bore into me, as though she has given me a dare.

"Remember, we are not discussing whether or not we like the piece. We're assuming that we're a team of editors who have accepted this piece for publication and we're just discussing ways to improve it. What stands out for us? What do we like?"

The compliments contradict each other.

The retired dentist likes knowing that seventy-five percent of babies born at twenty-five weeks have major disabilities. He says it gives him a sense of what the stakes are. But the middle school teacher finds it distracting. The journalist-turned-MFA-student agrees.

"I thought that about the technical terms and acronyms: ROP? PDA? NEC? Too much jargon makes my eyes glaze over. The narrative should be enough," she says, sticking a knife into the cream cheese and smearing it onto a sesame bagel.

I nod and take notes, wrinkling my brow with my best thoughtful-and-appreciative look. I like the technical terms but maybe I've overdone it. I'm here to learn.

"Well, the jargon kinda pulls us out of the emotional moment," chimes in the travel writer. "What I really want to know is, how does the narrator feel? What is she feeling when she's listening to this mother sobbing through the hospital walls?"

I open my mouth to speak. And then I clamp it shut, like a pet goldfish. I'm flipping back and forth, writing notes on my manuscript, places where people didn't get what I was trying to say.

"I was thinking," the travel writer continues, "that on the first page, when the narrator tells the doctor that looking at a twenty-six-week micro preemie is like looking at a car accident, that, well, that's a great indicator of this mother's character. This is someone who does not want to acknowledge what's going on. I want more of that."

I stop and blink. Wait. What? I *am* acknowledging what's going on. Right?

The middle school teacher nods and raises her hand. "I marked that, too. And I want to see that. I mean, maybe she dismisses the doctor with a hand gesture or something, but what is she feeling when she says that? It feels like something is missing."

"Well, maybe that's how she's telling us that she's in denial. I like it." It's my friend Dorothy. I can tell from her tone of voice that she's coming to my defense, but I'm confused. I wasn't in denial when I made the comment about the twenty-six-weeker to the doctor. I was just purposely pushing away information that scared me because I didn't want to deal with it.

Was I in denial?

Wait. Am I in denial now?

"So what I'm hearing is that we need to feel that our narrator is emotionally vulnerable," the workshop leader says to the group. They nod.

Emotionally vulnerable? Who wants that? My whole life I've worked very hard *not* to be emotionally vulnerable. As a ballet dancer, as a mother. It's the worst kind of weakness. That's the whole point of the essay—that you can bypass all that emotional stuff by just recording the happy memories. The way a dancer commits the choreographer's favorite steps to memory.

The middle school teacher looks down at her papers. She shakes her head and whispers. "I can't imagine what that was like."

"Me, either," says the travel writer. "It must have been awful. Can you imagine? Every day? Not knowing what was going to happen to these twins? I want to see that here on the page."

I feel as if I have walked into a classroom where they are speaking Egyptian. I thought we were going to speak English. The people around the table look like a conspiracy—a group who has just discovered that I am the only person here who doesn't realize what she went through.

"And she tells us that the babies are small, but how small? What did they look like?"

"I marked that, too!" says the MFA student.

What did my babies look like? I feel defiant now. They looked like fetuses, okay? They looked like babies-in-waiting, in transition. They were baggy where they should have been filled out and puffy where they shouldn't have been.

But it's not what they looked like that was so awful. What was so disconcerting was that they had no awareness. They were so vacant. So limp. Chiara made eye contact right out of the womb. The boys, on the other hand, responded reflexively, like mollusks. That's what made them seem inhuman. That's what was so incredible about the first time I held Wagner and he grasped my thumb. Or the time I put Michael back in his isolette and he started to cry.

I feel a twinge of compassion. For my babies, for Matt, for Chiara, for me. I thought I was so clever. I thought if I could manipulate my memory, shaping and sculpting the facts the way I'd pull and stretch my limbs through an adagio, emphasizing the beauty and pretending it was all effortless, I thought that if I could do that, then I would never feel the fear. Now I see it was just a coping mechanism. Maybe it was healthier and more productive than drinking myself under the table every night but I still have to face the music.

The NICU sucked.

The NICU really sucked.

I feel so stupid. Why did I think that controlling the narrative would make my brain forget that the babies I loved might die?

There is a loud honking noise and when everyone turns to me, I realize that I am the one making it.

All of sudden I'm in the middle of a storm. It comes out in dry heaves like something is roiling up inside of me and trying to get out. If, when the twins were born, I watched my body from above them, now I am so much inside my body that I'm not even aware of what it is doing. Are my eyes darting from left to right or have they rolled back into my head? I don't know. I feel completely out of control. My nose is running and I can't decide which is worse—to let snot run down my face or to wipe my nose with my sleeve like a six-year-old. I grab one of the paper towels I'd brought along with the bagels, and when I wipe my face I smear cream cheese on my cheek in the process.

"I'm sorry I'm crying," I croak. "I just realized that—oh, my God—the NICU sucked."

The workshop leader gives me a tender look. "Of course it did," she says, as if I have said, "There's no snow on the ground today."

I open my mouth to laugh but when the rush of laughter starts to erupt I feel the punch in my gut, the gravity of everything I have been pushing away.

The NICU totally sucked.

How did it feel?

I'm choking on air. I don't have a memory of remembering the NICU. I'm not picturing the boys in their isolettes. It's not a slide-show of NICU scenes. It's just a rush of dark emotions; it feels like black seawater. This is not like the radio interview where the interviewer talked about the dismal prognosis for the cognitive development of twenty-five-weekers, where I heard those stats and felt of a wave of fear like motion sickness. This is not like the countless hours I spent holding Michael or Wagner, skin-on-skin, smiling and peaceful. This is so much worse. All that time I spent spinning the story and squashing the emotions that I didn't want to digest. Oh my God. It's all coming back to me now.

I'm still crying when the session is over. Dorothy picks up the uneaten bagels and throws dirty napkins into the trash. One by one the other writers leave, patting me on the back as they hand copies of my words back to me. As the workshop leader leaves, she puts a hand on my shoulder and says something to me. But it's as if somebody put her on mute. I can't hear anything.

"Will you be okay?" Dorothy asks.

I nod. "I don't ever want to see another preemie as long as I live," I tell her.

And now the pictures come: Little pink wrinkled aliens who look like their skin is two sizes too big. Skinny babies who do not cry; they just turn their heads away, stretching their palms outward. Babies lying splayed on their backs or bundled up on their stomachs. Babies with tubes in their noses, down their throats, in their ankles. And I feel so sad that there is life trapped inside this skin, underneath these webs of blood vessels that are too thin and fragile to carry blood, inside lungs that can't stay open long enough to take a breath, behind a heart that has too much blood in one chamber and not enough in the others. A life force that is vibrant and a brain that is too mushy to tell the other organs what to do and when to do it.

I feel so sad for that mother—me—standing over them, pushing away her feelings and telling jokes instead.

But now, I remind myself, the boys are at their daycare. Maybe they'll fall asleep holding hands again. My slideshow of helpless baggy aliens is replaced by the boys as I remembered them last week—Wagner with graham cracker crumbs all over his face. Michael taking a paper towel and wiping down his high chair tray. Their fascination with empty cereal boxes and spatulas. Their recent discovery that drawers can be opened and contents can be dumped on the floor. Their contagious laughter and peek-a-boo games with each other. The cardboard boxes they wear as hats. The sheer joy at the sound of a double-axle vehicle making its way down the street because chances are it's a garbage truck! This is where I want to be. Is this just denial again? I'm too exhausted to sort it out.

It's just me and the mountain now. It stands there, exposed and proud. The wind blows a piece of trash across the parking lot. A bird chirps. It sounds so clear, as if my ears have just been tuned. Even the echo of my footsteps sounds crisp.

⋆　⋆　⋆　⋆　⋆

The writing workshop concludes with The Follies. There are songs and monologues, funny routines such as the soufflé recipe read in the manner of a Beat poet by the program director. I put my name in the hat to perform. For the first time since I had children, I will dance in front of an audience. I'll dance The Dying Swan variation. I don't particularly want to dance this dated, melodramatic ballerina solo, but it's the only music on my iPod that fits the requirement of being shorter than three minutes.

The premise of this short dance is simple: at the beginning a swan is flapping her wings; two minutes and forty seconds later she's dead. That's why they call it *The Dying Swan*. I had planned to dance a simplified version of the traditional choreography I'd first learned in Iceland from Eva Evdokimiva. But after yesterday's workshop the dance has taken on a different purpose.

I have been so overwhelmed by the emotions that keep pushing their way to the surface I can't string sentences together. I'm shocked to discover that the NICU was so traumatizing and I'm embarrassed that I tried so hard to delude myself. At the same time I'm relieved to finally admit that I'm grieving. But mostly I just feel sad. Crushingly, wind-knocked-out-of-me sad. I'm sad for the past that I tried to push away. I'm sad for the future because we don't know what's ahead for us.

I didn't think to bring ballet shoes (why would I?) so I'll be dancing in bare feet. I didn't think to bring a costume, either, but luckily I have a party dress, black with bright green stripes and silver beadwork that works nicely. When it's my turn to dance, I hand my iPod to the program director's son, a young teenager who doubles as a roadie for the performance. I take my place facing upstage, away from the audience. Through the huge floor-to-ceiling windows of the main room that was once the Olympic Lodge for the 1960 Winter Olympics, I can see the mountain.

Yesterday it looked so exposed and vulnerable without snow. Today it just looks like a mountain. Next week when I go home to Oakland, instead of spinning stories and reframing statistics, I will write what I remember. I will remember scenes from the NICU such as leaving the boys' hospital room every twenty minutes. How I'd lock myself in the bathroom for three minutes of "nerve-strengthening" breathing exercises I'd learned when I taught yoga to ballet dancers.

I'll remember the soap of the NICU. How every Tuesday when we'd meet with the early intervention specialists, I'd wash my hands and breathe in the chemical-orange scent. It had smelled like victory. It will suddenly occur to me that the last time we went, I washed my hands and the familiar odor made my gut twist. The smell had soured for me. I'll remember how the twins' earlobes folded over, like the corners of a dinner napkin.

I will remember thinking, "I don't want your explanations. I want a crystal ball." I will remember shoving something down inside me, something that felt like rage.

Letting myself remember will feel like guiding myself down a cold tunnel inch by inch, like the ones in the New Mexico caverns we would visit when I was a child. It was cold and the air felt thin, ancient, devoid of life, like the air in outer space. There was a path but it felt like we didn't know where we were going. And then we'd turn the corner and see something beautiful—ancient stalactites and mounds of limestone stalagmites.

But I'm not ready for that yet. Tonight I am just feeling.

The first notes are the piano arpeggios. But I wait for the cello to begin the dance, connecting the vibration of its sigh to my center of gravity, feeling the silvery music ripple through my arms and legs.

I wish someone had told me this secret when I was a young dancer: onstage, facial expressions do not express emotion. Expression is actually a telepathic connection between dancer and audience. It's not enough to look happy or scared. But if I remember a time when I felt terrified and replay that memory as I dance, the feeling will permeate my movement and the audience will sense that I'm scared. I might not know how to be emotionally vulnerable on the page, but I do know how to dance it in front of two hundred people.

My feet mirror the patter of piano keys as my arms wave, simulating both the wings of a bird and the bow of the cello. The tiny steps of the choreography feel like a panic that is contradicted by the flutter of my dancer's wings. In my interpretation the swan knows she's dying. She resists death briefly but does not grasp for life. Her dance is a reconciliation, a resignation, and finally, total acceptance.

My jaw goes slack and my shoulders broaden—like wings. I don't have to fight tears the way I did in the NICU, digging my nails into my palms or trying to imagine swallowing an apple. I can let the emotions move like a shudder through my limbs. I can work with gravity, not against it. I feel the eye of the storm in the pit of my stomach, and at one point I balance on the ball of one foot. Ten, eleven, twelve counts.

Every time I feel the urge to retreat or push away my feelings, I take a deep breath and feel the tension that emanates from the audience. It's unlikely they are feeling what I'm feeling, but that doesn't matter. Their attention becomes a lifeline, a conduit. Somehow, the fact that this expression of grief is public makes it feel that much more genuine.

Colors reverberate from my heart through my fingertips as cello and piano sing together in surround sound. Waves of magenta, streaks of light turquoise, canary yellow swirls, dark black splotches, and then finally, colorless.

When the swan takes her last breath in the final bars of the music, I have said everything I needed to say.

It feels so good to finally exhale.

25

FINAL BOW

Overhead a red helicopter flies to Children's Hospital. It's loud and we stop to watch it. We are walking to the flower stand to get flowers for Daddy. Matt is coming home today, just in time for Easter. He has spent the last week in Tampa with his parents now that his father is in hospice.

"Copter!" Michael shrieks with delight.

"Where's it going?" Chiara asks.

Six months ago I would have invented an answer to avoid talking about hospitals and the children who need to be airlifted to them. But after attending the writing workshop in Tahoe I am trying to call things the way they are, even if it makes me feel uncomfortable. Sometimes it's a relief to say, "Yes, that's an awful thing" and sometimes it's not. But at least I'm not trying to twist the truth anymore, and that feels good. Especially now, knowing that Grandpa is in his last weeks of life. I need to practice repeating age-appropriate explanations about sickness and death. The boys are still too young, but Chiara knows that Grandpa is very sick.

"That helicopter is going to Children's Hospital. That's where

Wagner went last summer when the ambulance came to help us." At the mention of his name, Wagner looks at us. He is chewing some bark he has found in a neighbor's yard. I hold out my hand and he spits it out. Michael is barely willing to eat crackers and plain pasta but Wagner is a true omnivore. Lasagna, yogurt, guacamole, pinecones, you name it. Bark is his latest delicacy.

"I bet that little kid's mama is scared," Chiara concludes. "And I bet that little kid's daddy is scared, too."

I nod. This is what we are practicing—telling our five-year-old that it's okay to be scared.

"And if that little kid has a brother or sister, then I bet that brother or sister is scared, too," she continues. "And the little kid's Grandpa, if that Grandpa is still alive."

"Yes. They are probably worried," I concede. "But I'm glad they are at the hospital now. The doctors and nurses will work their hardest to help that little kid." My voice cracks as I speak. I wonder if the mother is in the helicopter with her child or if she has to drive herself to the hospital. I wonder if her gut is twisting as she tries to be strong in this place of uncertainty.

At the flower stand Chiara selects blossoms for Matt's bouquet—all pink. Meanwhile, Wagner eyes the baby's breath, no doubt wondering if it is edible.

"My Daddy's coming home today!" Chiara tells the florist.

"Oh! Where is he now?"

"Florida."

"On vacation?" the florist wraps the collection of fuchsia roses and coral pink carnations in brown paper and hands them to her.

"No. My Grandpa has cancer," Chiara says matter-of-factly, taking the flower arrangement.

The woman looks ashen. I smile weakly. Honesty is harder than I thought it would be.

"I'm so sorry," the woman finally stutters.

"It's okay," I answer. It feels like a dumb thing to say but I can't think of anything better. That's the other thing about honesty—it's often awkward.

On our walk home Chiara has more questions.

"Is Grandpa going to get better?"

I suck in my breath. The preschool has preemptively given us books on this topic to help us discuss the cycle of life but taken off guard like this, I can't remember anything I've read.

"No," I answer plainly.

"Is Grandpa going to die?"

"Yes," I say, biting my lip.

Chiara nods for a bit. "That will make us sad."

"Yes, it will," I say.

She smells her flowers.

"Mama?"

"Yes, honey?"

"Can I take ballet classes?"

The train of thought in a five-year-old child's brain seems like a game of hopscotch, jumping from uncertainty to sadness to dancing.

I smile and stroke her hair. "Yes, sweetie. Yes, you can. We can go to the studio right now and sign up."

Maybe, I think to myself, I'll ask if they need a ballet teacher.

* * * * *

We are napping on the couch when Matt gets the call that his father has passed. Matt's phone, which has been returned to its place in his pajama pocket, buzzes us awake. We knew this day was coming, but it still takes us by surprise. The boys' miraculous health had lulled us into hoping that Mike would make a similar recovery. A few days from now we will hug friends and family and say things such as, "It happened much too soon," and, "At least he's not in pain anymore." But today we just sit in silence, letting the sadness envelop us like a golden umbrella.

That night Chiara hands us one of the books gifted to her from her preschool teachers. The book, through cartoon dinosaurs, describes death in a child-appropriate way.

Matt begins reading: "Losing someone who is special to you is very hard to understand. When someone you love dies, there is no right or wrong way to feel."

Every page depicts cartoon scenes of life and death: the burial of a pet, a sick parent, a car accident, a memorial service for the Grandpa dinosaur, "Morris Saurus." There is even a cartoon panel with two little baby dinosaur preemies hooked up to tubes and wires in little incubators.

"Just like the boys!" Chiara exclaims, recognizing the NICU equipment even in dinosaur cartoons.

"Yes, the boys are healthy now, but they were very little and sick when they were born," I tell her. "We loved them very much, but we were also very scared."

"We should give this book to Grandma," she says. "So she won't be so sad about Grandpa."

Matt smiles but his eyes are sad. "That's a good idea."

After we finish reading, we play the game suggested on one of the last pages: "I remember when . . ."

"I remember when Grandpa came to visit and read books to you," I begin.

"I remember Grandpa's birthday party," she says.

"I remember when we hiked Mount Shasta," says Matt.

"I remember the cards he used to make for us."

I used to think I could manipulate my emotions by only committing the happy scenes of my life to memory—the onstage triple pirouette in Reykjavik, dancing with Matt at our wedding, tickling Chiara when she was a baby. I thought that I didn't need to reconcile the past in order to enjoy the middle. I was wrong. Scary memories were like shadows nipping at my heels and I was afraid that remembering them would be the same as reliving them. It would be debilitating. I didn't realize that shadows—maybe even metaphorical ones, too—change with the light, but they go away in the dark. Remembering is reconciliation.

We do a few more rounds of "I Remember When" before it's time to say goodnight. Tomorrow she has ballet class. We both do.

Later, sitting in the living room, Matt and I play "I Remember the NICU." He starts.

"I remember sitting in those pink rocking chairs, each of us holding a baby."

"They were peach-colored. Not pink. I remember when your dad sent fudge for the nurses."

"I remember we kept some of that fudge for ourselves," he chuckles.

My voice lowers. "I remember looking at those pictures for the first time. The ones taken right after they were born."

Matt nods. "I remember that, too. My wedding ring would have fit on Michael's wrist."

"Remember how you wanted to popularize 'nee-COO' instead of NICU?"

Matt laughs. "I still think that sounds better."

26

A NEW STAGE

The boys' final developmental NICU checkups are scheduled to coincide with the magic period when their chronological age merges with their adjusted age. Milestones are calculated in ranges—monthly for infants, in three-month periods for toddlers, and six months for preschoolers. At twenty-nine months Michael and Wagner are on the cusp. This evaluation will decide whether we can think of them as two-year-olds or two-and-a-half-year olds.

Each time we visited the NICU follow-up clinic in the past, I'd hoped to walk out with a gold medal, an engraved accolade we could hang over the fireplace: Most Amazing Micro Preemies Ever. Instead we'd walk out with handouts and referrals for early intervention specialists and pediatric audiologists.

This time I don't care how we measure up. I don't think of the evaluation as a test the boys need to pass but as an indication of what they know and what we need to work on. If the boys need extra support, we'll give them support. Just the same way that, if our boys had needed hearing aids, then we would have gotten them hearing aids.

Because the examination spans three hours, Matt and I have opted to test the boys on different days. Michael goes first. His June appointment is scheduled for the day that would have been Grandpa Mike's seventy-second birthday.

It's very low-tech—nothing like the EEG test at Children's Hospital. But Michael is so still, so serious, as if this is NASA headquarters and he is interviewing to be an astronaut. Is he so still and serious because he remembers these sorts of tests? Or is he just well practiced from Chiara's days of playing doctor? He doesn't look like a child. He looks like a little grownup who is waiting for a train.

All of sudden I feel very sad. Maybe this is just how Matt and I make kids—kids who often sit still. Or maybe Michael is a little sentient being who has always known that big people are testing, looking for measurable indications that eventually will indicate that we can stop measuring.

"Hi, Michael. I'm Dr. Nancy and I have some games to play. Do you want to play some games today, Michael?"

Michael stares intently at Dr. Nancy, as if he's thinking, "Game on, lady." But he says nothing.

Dr. Nancy has a big fat binder of test questions and a bag of props. She's quick. Her hands move with the speed of an experienced magician. One hand records Michael's response while the other moves on to the next test. It's dizzying. I wonder if, at the end of the appointment, she will pull a pink referral form out of my ear the way nightclub illusionists pull out coins. As she flips through the pages asking questions, "Can you find the bears? Where are the bears?" she scribbles down Michael's answers.

I'm not sure what Michael is thinking, but it's a good thing he doesn't have telekinetic powers because he's shooting Dr. Nancy the sort of look that could make her burst into flames. Either Dr. Nancy doesn't notice or she knows that Micro Preemie Michael is no *Carrie*.

"Look at this chip, Michael," she says, holding up a blue plastic medallion. "Do you see a color like that here?" She brushes the chip over a page of six basic colors. Michael points to the blue circle.

"How about this chip? Do you see this chip, Michael?"

The task is repeated five more times. Michael answers every question correctly. Dr. Nancy raises her eyebrows.

"We don't expect them to recognize colors by name at this age." She makes a note.

I am less impressed. After all, this is the Red Baby. He's always had orange or red dishes while his brother, the Blue Baby gets blue or green. Colors have always been important. And whether Michael really does gravitate toward red things or he is just a product of his red environment, he knew his colors before he knew I was "Mama."

The next test is to feed a doll.

"Would you like a baby, Michael? This is your baby. Can you feed your baby?" Dr. Nancy gives him a doll and a bottle.

Michael just grins at her. He doesn't know that he's been given a task.

"Can you feed your doll, Michael? Like this? I'm going to feed my baby doll. Look!" She feeds her doll.

Michael continues to grin, holding his doll with the maternal affection one displays with a dishcloth or a potato.

Dr. Nancy repeats her request again. And again.

Feed the doll, Michael. I feel the same urgency and helplessness of a fan watching her favorite baseball player take a called strike. *I know you can do it.*

The doctor retrieves a doll-sized soccer ball from her bag of tricks. "Can you make your doll kick the ball?"

Michael's grin breaks into a wide smile. He makes his baby doll kick the ball over to Dr. Nancy. Goooooooalllll! Next to me, Matt smiles with pride.

"OOH! Good, Michael. Let's play another game, Michael. Do you want to play another one of my games?"

With a sweep of her hand the binder disappears and Dr. Nancy sets up three empty cups.

"See these pegs? Can you put the pegs in the cups?"

It's a task within a task. The first is to understand the instructions and follow them. The second is to sort the red, yellow, and blue pegs according to color, although Dr. Nancy doesn't explicitly give this instruction. She doesn't expect him to do it correctly, either. The task, I find out later, is a developmental milestone for three-year-olds. He is only expected to put the pegs in the cups. I am not surprised in the slightest when Michael sorts the colors. Michael is obsessed with order. He cleans up drops of water that fall on the sidewalk. When his brother has an accident, he gets a towel to wipe pee off the floor. When he washes his hands, he makes sure he lines up his stool parallel with the edge of the counter. I was the same way as a kid. As was my mother and my grandfather.

Dr. Nancy moves to test language skills.

"Michael," Dr. Nancy asks. Her cheery falsetto never wavers. "Can you put the block *in* the cup?"

Michael puts the block in the cup.

Dr. Nancy turns the cup over.

"Michael, can you put the block *on* the cup?"

Michael puts the block on the cup.

Dr. Nancy puts the cup right-side-up again and asks, "Michael, can you put the block *against* the cup?"

Michael jerks to attention and shoots Dr. Nancy a hard look.

"It's okay, Michael," Dr. Nancy says soothingly. She repeats her request. "Can you put the block *against* the cup? Can you show me?"

Michael gives Dr. Nancy another funny look. Then he picks up the block and with all the force of a small person with the gross motor skills of a twenty-nine-month-old uses it to whack the cup off the table. Dr. Nancy raises an eyebrow.

"Okaaaaay. So we know you understand the preposition *against*," she wryly notes. Matt and I look at each other and grin.

I can tell by the way Dr. Nancy records Michael's answers that he is doing better than expected. I know that when you flunk the tests, the doctors sit very still with their best poker faces, trying not to give anything away. Just in the hour that we have been here, Dr. Nancy has softened.

There are few tasks Michael does not do correctly. For example, he has no idea what to do with the scissors he is handed and he is unable to identify a vacuum cleaner, which I suppose reflects more on me than it does on him.

Dr. Nancy points to a picture of a little girl at a park with a ball at her feet.

"What's happening in this picture, Michael? Can you tell me what's happening here?"

She's looking for a simple subject-verb-object sentence: "Girl kick ball."

Michael points to the card. "She's playing soccer," he says without hesitation. A pronoun, a contraction, a present participle, and the ability to identify a soccer ball.

Dr. Nancy nods and shuts the binder. "I think we're done here. Your son speaks on the level of a three-and-a-half-year-old. I'll see you next week with Wagner, but if he's anything like his brother, you don't ever have to come back here."

Through the mysterious metrics of developmental testing, Wagner scores just as highly as his brother even though he answers incorrectly half the time. Perhaps he received extra credit for his enthusiasm.

"Right there!" he exclaims, pointing happily to the airplane when he is supposed to point at the car.

"Right there!" to the car when he should have pointed at the bus.

His sentences are just as complex as Michael's, however, and when presented with a picture of a girl in mid-yawn he says, "She's getting ready to go to sleep."

Dr. Nancy counts the words on her fingers. Seven. And just like that Michael and Wagner are not preemies anymore. "When they go to kindergarten, don't even tell the school about their prematurity unless you want to brag."

Matt and I can hardly believe it. We should celebrate, but we are too stunned. A part of me feels unsettled, even a little angry, the way a mother yells at her child after he has been lost in a crowded supermarket and then found, yelling at him because he is okay and she was so worried.

"Two and a half years ago we thought they might have to be fed through a synthetic stomach port," Matt whispers as we walk back to the car. "Remember that?"

I laugh but it sounds like a scoff. I anthropomorphize the NICU as a big floating Macy's parade balloon with a sinister face, something that has been shadowing us. I want the whole thing to not have any meaning at all. To not bear any more weight on the future than my choice to switch to drinking cappuccinos instead of lattes.

"They didn't even weigh Wagner. He refused to take off his shoes so they just wrote down Michael's weight from last week."

Matt laughs. It's genuine and it makes me laugh, too. No more hearing tests. No more early intervention specialists. No more visits to an occupational therapist. We're done. We're not preemies anymore.

★ ★ ★ ★ ★

It doesn't take long for us to get used to our new status as "not preemies" and it's as if our appointment with Dr. Nancy has opened the floodgates—the boys chatter from morning to night.

"Where's my fire truck?"

"I like breakfast."

"You want ice cream, Mama?"

"No, Mama! I do it!"

"Dat's Light-neen McQueen!"

"Where's Thomas?"

"Let's run together, Wag-nah."

"I don't wanna run together."

"Don't touch da poop, Wag-nah."

"Mic-cull mad. I happy!"

"My dump truck has a red ball innit."

"My pants dry!"

"I no have to go potty. I 'ready went."

They know things now. Things I don't even know, such as the difference between a backhoe and an excavator. Where I see one creepy cartoon train, they see four different characters: Gordon, Thomas, Percy, and Bertie.

"Whooz-zat?" Wagner lifts his arms to be picked up. He points to the picture on the refrigerator that apparently he has never noticed before. It's a photo from the NICU. I'm holding Michael on my chest. His tiny arms are folded and his cheek rests on the back of his hands. He looks like one of Michelangelo's cherubs.

Wagner points to the tubes in Michael's nose. "What's on dat baby's face?"

Suddenly it occurs to me that I will have to tell him that he was very little when he was born.

"That's Michael. Those tubes are there to help him breathe. Do you know 'breathe?' Can you breathe?" I don't know if Wagner knows what the word "breathe" means. I inhale loudly through my nose to demonstrate. He sniffs loudly.

"Where's Wag-nah?" he demands.

I show him another picture from the refrigerator. Wagner is a month old in this photo. His eyes are closed. Unlike Michael's photo, Wagner's breathing tube leads directly into his lungs through his mouth, secured by that damn tape. His hair is blond and he still has a bit of toaster head. Wagner studies the picture. If he notices anything strange or scary, he doesn't show it.

"This is my favorite picture," I tell him, and I take a third photograph from the fridge. It curls up at the edges and is starting to fade. In it, Michael and Wagner are tightly swaddled cheek-to-cheek. The tubes are thinner; the tape is wider. They are nearly three months old, but they are still in the NICU. Their eyes are closed and swollen but to the untrained eye, it just looks like baby fat. Michael looks as if he is smiling, as though there is no happier place on earth than next to his twin brother. This, too, is part of the story.

27

BACK IN THE STUDIO

Seven little kindergarten-aged girls in pale pink tights and pastel pink leotards sit in a circle and mimic my stretching.

"Point your feet. Straighten your knees! Can you touch your toes?" I reach toward my feet. Chiara and her friends do the same. Music from *Coppeliá* plays in the background. If Chiara remembers it from the performance we saw together when she was three years old, she doesn't show it. To her, it's just the music she stretches to on Wednesdays, the same stretches I did after the boys were born.

"Everyone to the corner. Can you dance like a butterfly?"

We dance to *The Dying Swan* music too, except in my class it's called "The Fancy Butterfly." My students take their improvisation seriously. Pink chiffon skirts billow and float around their tiny waists as they leap and turn, completely uninhibited.

When my brain is still—that is, when I'm not figuring out which snacks all three kids will eat or making sure that the twins aren't climbing the bookcases—I am dancing. I don't know exactly when it happened, but sometime after performing *The Dying Swan* in Tahoe I stopped executing *brisés* to the right and the left and the right and the left. These days when I'm dancing in my head, it's to the music of *Coppélia*—Swanhilda's opening solo. It's not the choreography I learned from Eva Evdokimiva; instead, the choreography I dance is different every time. I never stop-action the mental video to correct myself; I just dance, free and unconstrained, the way my five-year-old butterflies dance.

"I think today our butterflies should be butterfly fairies. What do you think?"

The class cheers. Fairy roles are always accompanied with wands. The seven little girls crowd around me as I rummage through a drawer of studio props and hand out silver wands with star-shaped tips.

At the bottom of the drawer, under tie-dyed scarves and glow sticks, is a pair of white satin Freeds. The shoes are brand new without ribbons or elastics. I don't need to read the name in block letters under Maker C's stamp to recognize the shape of the vamp and cut of the cloth. Of course my shoes would find their way here. The sheen on the ivory satin is still shiny. The black specks are barely visible. If you didn't think to look for the imperfections, you might not even see them.

ACKNOWLEDGMENTS

I started writing this story in 2009 as soon as I found out that I was carrying monoamniotic-monochorionic twins. Even then I imagined it as a book, but only because I didn't understand the Herculean efforts and community involvement required to bring a book into the world. Luckily for me, I met many wonderful and talented writers and editors over the last eight years. I am so grateful for their vision, guidance, and support.

First of all, thank you to the Write on Mamas for welcoming me into your ranks and making me feel like this writing thing was a reasonable goal. I'm not sure if the word "inclusivity" was in vogue yet, but it was certainly already part of the group's special sauce.

To the Community of Writers at Squaw Valley, especially Brett Hall Jones, Sands Hall, and Lisa Alvarez, thank you for the workshops, the Follies, the hard-boiled eggs, and creating a communal space where we can all rejoice over the process rather than obsess over the product. Thank you to Mimi and Burnett Miller for the 2011 George Pascoe Miller Memorial Scholarship, to Michael Carlisle for the 2012 Carlisle Family Scholarship, and to Dirk Eshleman for the Eshleman Scholarship in 2014. Your generosity made it possible for me to attend. Thank you to Dorothy O'Donnell, Marianne Lonsdale, Cyndi Cady, Andy Dugas, Ian Tuttle, Alia Volz, Joy Johannessen, Jason Roberts, Anika Streitfeld, Robin Romm, Dava Sobel, Mary Evans, and Leslie Daniels for your encouragement and words of wisdom.

To Jack Boulware, Jane Ganahl, and the Litquake Foundation: you are shining examples of how to take creative risks and foster community and I'm grateful to be along for the ride. Plus, you serve wine at meetings.

Kate Hopper, I came for the workshop and the promise of my own room with a fireplace; I return for the friendship. Thank you for all of it.

For my Wednesday Sisters—Rachel Sarah, Alexandra Ballard, Angelisa Russo, and Jill Smith Dempster—thank you for the gentle reminders that stories from the ballet world are more entertaining than cognitive science lessons. And as I tried to weave those stories together, thank you to Jane Hodges and the Mineral School for the gift of residency. Two weeks with a view of Mt. Rainier from my desk yielded the first complete and nearly coherent draft of this manuscript.

Residencies are addictive, and I am grateful to Hedgebrook for the opportunity to stay in Willow Cottage and the Meadow House. Your radical hospitality is like writer's manna. To my Slug Sister cohort: Dionne Ford, Celeste Gainey, Naomi Williams, Sara Nović, and Xochitl-Julisa Bermejo, you are always welcome at the Manor. I'll even give you your own bathrobes.

Thank you to Elizabeth George and the Elizabeth George Foundation for the financial gift that became the initial investment that allowed this book to come into being. Thank you for your generous support for emerging writers.

This book would not exist without the patience and persistence of Mary Hill and Joanne Hartman. Your edits and suggestions improved each revision. I am so grateful for your guidance, your friendship, the late-night texts, the fresh pasta, and frozen chocolate zucchini bread. #brainshare.

This book would also not exist without the talents of Cary Tennis, Jamie L. Real, Dr. Roberta Ballard, Vicki DeArmon, Alicia Feltman,

Laurel Hilton, Terry Lorant and Pete Jacobson. Thank you for being part of the village. Beth Hoge, Claudine Naganuma, and KT Mower, thank you for making Danspace our home next door to home. Tarja Parssinen, you make it look easy. Thank you for your quick wit, your contagious enthusiasm, and your words of encouragement. I can't wait to see where Moxie Road Productions will take us next.

To the doctors and nurses who saved our boys' lives, we are forever indebted to you. Thank you for all you do on behalf of NICU babies and their families. Alison Brooks, thank you for always asking for another story. I am happy to comply and always tickled that you ask.

None of this would have been possible without the support of my family. To my parents, Phoebe and Elroy Bode, Jerry and Marian Bryan, you have supported me through three careers and counting. Thank you for always believing that I could. Thank you for standing by our side at the NICU, for taking our kids to the park and to the pool and for braving the road trips in between. Mom (aka "Nonna Extraordinaire") and Elroy, you read every sentence in this manuscript multiple times, backwards and forwards. You counted commas and noted misspellings. Your eagle eyes made this a tighter manuscript. And I'm so very grateful (see what I did there?)

To Mike and Midge Kovac, the best in-laws I could imagine. To my brothers, sister, and sisters in-law: Jason, Jeff, Jackie, Jess, and Liz—you cook dinners, read stories, and take care of our children as if they were your own. You ride roller coasters with us, literally and figuratively. I'm so happy to know you in this life, and I love you all.

To my wonderful children, Chiara, Michael, and Wagner—you fill my life with love, laughter, and LEGO sets.

Finally, to Matt, when I do the math, I realize there was a time when we didn't dance together but I can't remember what that was like. Thank you for living this with me. And for always doing the dishes. I love you. Strap in. Let's open some windows.

ABOUT THE AUTHOR

JANINE KOVAC was a soloist with The National Ballet of Iceland (*Íslenski Dansflokkurinn*). Her career included dancing for companies in Italy, Austria, San Francisco, and in her hometown of El Paso, Texas. After ballet, Janine worked as a database architect and software engineer. She is a founding member of the 501(c)(3) nonprofit writing group Write on Mamas and co-founder of Moxie Road Productions, a consulting firm that helps women bring their ideas into the world. Janine is the author of *Brain Changer: A Mother's Guide to Cognitive Science* and a contributing editor of the anthology *Mamas Write: 29 Tales of Truth, Wit, and Grit*. In 2016 she was awarded the Elizabeth George Foundation Fellowship from Hedgebrook in addition to the gift of residency. She lives in Oakland, California, with her family.

ALSO BY
JANINE KOVAC

Brain Changer: A Mother's Guide to Cognitive Science

ANTHOLOGIES

Mamas Write: 29 Tales of Truth, Wit, and Grit

Tiny Feet, Giant Steps: Portraits of Miracles in the Alta Bates Summit Newborn Intensive Care Unit

Multiples Illuminated: A Collection of Stories and Advice from Parents of Twins, Triplets, and More

The Book of Kid: Parenting Advice from Third Graders (editor)